MY STORY

Bringing Beverly Back From The Brink...

William F. Scanlon
Former, and longest serving mayor
of Beverly, Massachusetts

© Copyright 2022 by William F. Scanlon

All rights reserved. No part of this publication may be reproduced, distributed or transmitted in any form or by any means, without prior written permission.

William F. Scanlon/Beverly Historical Society
117 Cabot Street
Beverly MA 01915
historicbeverly.net

My Story: Bringing Beverly Back From The Brink
Printed in the United States of America
ISBN: 978-1-891906-09-1

This book is dedicated to the citizens of Beverly who believed in me and put their trust in me at the ballot box on nine separate occasions, creating the opportunity to "Bring Beverly Back From The Brink."

CONTENTS

Introduction 1

An Appreciated Thank You 5

The Early Years 9

College, the Military and Graduate School 13

Going to Work 19

Restructuring the Massive Beverly Operation 25

Worldwide Responsibility 33

The Sudden End 35

A Change in Lifestyle 37

My Entry Into Politics 39

My First Years in Office 47

Some Last Minute Opposition 61

Losing, Teaching, Then Winning Again 69

Back At It in Tough Times 75

Another Surprise Opponent 87

Lots of Good News 89

My Last Hurrah 93

Special Tributes 101

Photo Essay 105

Acknowledgments 121

MY STORY

Bringing Beverly Back From The Brink...

William F. Scanlon

Introduction

Bill Scanlon, a man with absolutely no political experience, was elected mayor of the City of Beverly, Massachusetts in November 1993, sweeping to victory in every precinct in each ward in the city. The citizens of Beverly had had enough of the five-term mayor, Jack Monahan.

Beverly, a city of over 40,000 people, was in dire straits and appeared headed for receivership. The city had run up bills for millions of dollars with no means to pay those bills. Beverly's bond rating had been trashed to "junk" status. Beverly's Community Development Office had been closed by the state for malfeasance. Beverly had become a joke across the Commonwealth of Massachusetts. The city was being lampooned in magazines with cartoons comparing its management to the then popular "Beverly Hillbillies" TV series.

Specifically, the city had created a deficit over $8,000,000. A deficit is created by spending money one does not have, the equivalent of cashing bad checks on a large scale, spending the proceeds and then having to make restitution with no means to do so.

I am Bill Scanlon, and this is my story. I was born in 1940, growing up in Dorchester, a blue-collar section of Boston. My father was a wholesale meat salesman, my mother a housewife. While my story largely unfolds in chronological order there is some information that I wish to share with the reader at the outset.

In 1974 I was transferred by my employer to Beverly, tasked with restructuring the city's biggest business, resulting in the largest layoff in Beverly's history. Many hundreds of good and faithful employees lost their jobs through no fault of their own. It was a tumultuous time.

Nearly twenty years later, in 1993, I was elected mayor of Beverly at a critical time in the city's history. What follows are highlights of events that occurred in the weeks between that election and my being sworn in, plus what happened in the first few weeks I was mayor.

In the intervening weeks between the November 1993 election and the January oath taking, I traveled frequently to Boston, the state capitol, apologizing to any state official (who would listen) for my predecessor's insulting and acrimonious behavior. Beverly had become persona non grata with government officials. In one case I was berated by a state attorney who had witnessed the former mayor "savaging" the lady in charge of the state's Local Revenue Department that was responsible for all monetary transactions between municipalities and state government. That was a very low point. It still sticks in my mind. There was nothing to do but apologize profusely and promise much better behavior from my administration and myself.

The visits to officials in Boston were an effort to reopen the door to various state funds badly needed by our city and to make clear that complete cooperation could be expected from Beverly officials from then on.

Only a few days after being installed as mayor, I sat in my office looking at an invoice in my left hand from the South Essex Sewage District, a regional entity that processes all of Beverly's effluent. That invoice had been in Beverly's possession since the previous April and covered the entire fiscal year from July 1, 1993 to June 30, 1994. In my right hand I held a copy of the city's annual budget for the same fiscal year. The problem was that the invoice was for exactly $600,000 more than what the city had budgeted to cover that cost. That budget had been prepared by the then mayor and his finance director —well after receipt of the invoice — and had been approved by the nine-member City Council during the previous June. Incidentally, six of the nine council members were voted out of office in the subsequent November election, the same one in which I was first elected. The underfunding was not a mistake. It was a deliberate act on the part of the mayor and his finance director to hide bad news until after the November election. All the councilors were aware, or should have been aware, of the skulduggery. In Massachusetts, state law requires that the annual operating budget of every city and town must balance each fiscal year. There are no ifs, ands, or buts. That is the law.

That was my welcome to office, or more correctly, part of it. I also learned that in the last few days of 1993 between Christmas and New Years, just before I was sworn into office, the members of the Municipal Golf and Tennis Commission, a group of citizen volunteers, and the departing mayor had awarded a five-year binding contract extension to the current municipal golf course operator. That extension continued the practice of the city receiving only a pittance in annual revenue from the golf course, well below what the operator should have been paying. Had the contract been put out to bid, competitive operators would have offered significant six-figure annual payments.

The arrangement was cozy. In return for a non-competitive contract, commission members were treated royally. I later dubbed two of them the King and the Prince of the golf course. They had informal power and swagger the likes of which presidents of private golf courses would envy, always the best of tee times, free guest privileges, you name it. They had stuck it to me. It would be five years before I could get golf course revenues to the city up to a reasonable level. Meanwhile, the city would derive peanuts from this valuable asset at a cost of more than $1,000,000 lost. This contract was a major hit to a city that needed every dime of revenue.

When walking into problems like the two I have described, one has to be suspicious of everything. What and whom can you trust? I have a cardinal rule in turnaround situations — the kind of work I have done for much of my life — to make as few personnel changes as possible, especially at the beginning. Get to know what your department heads know. Give them a chance to perform. Learn where the bones are buried so to speak. Even if you are sure that the City Finance Director will have to be terminated one day, and I was sure, take your time and learn his secrets.

In the case of the golf course there was nothing I could do, not now. Fortunately, the sewage funding issue was different. It is true that Massachusetts cities and towns raise most of their funds through real estate taxes. It is also true that a state law known as Proposition 2-1/2 limits the overall annual real estate tax increase on established properties to 2-1/2 percent. Individual properties may differ, but the overall average cannot exceed the 2-1/2 percent.

Fortunately, water and sewer costs by law do not fall under the umbrella of Prop 2-1/2 and can be legislated locally. Analysis of the sewer rate question revealed that in addition to the $600,000 problem, South Essex Sewage District costs to handle Beverly's effluent would increase by another million dollars for the new fiscal year to begin in July 1994. When all relevant factors were considered, it would be necessary to increase the

Beverly sewer rate by fifty-eight percent. Even with that increase Beverly's rate would be lower than that of several neighboring communities.

In short order I presented legislation to the City Council to increase the sewer rate that was quickly and unanimously approved. At this time in 1994 there were two full time newspaper reporters assigned to City Hall, one for the Beverly Times, the other for the Salem News. The sewer rate subject was closely followed in the newspapers. It turns out that Peter Torigian, mayor of the nearby City of Peabody, was also following the matter.

I had met Torigian but didn't know him well. He had a terrific reputation and had been elected many times. When the rate increase was approved he called me and stated that he was pleased that I was taking my job very seriously. That began a long and close relationship between the two of us. He educated me on many matters over the years and was a source of very useful advice. He became a true friend.

What you have read thus far is a taste of how my time in office began. There is much to be said about what we accomplished over nine terms, totaling eighteen years, including discussion of a few bloopers. There is also something to be said about my unlikely election in the first place and the attitude I brought with me to the job given my deep involvement in the massive layoffs of so many Beverly citizens two decades earlier.

As mayor I would have a chance to improve things, to do some good, to make Beverly a better place, to put the city on a healthy financial trajectory and to always take the long view of the city's best interests in making decisions. I wanted very much to make the most of the opportunity.

My story now shifts to a chronology of my life, ultimately describing the record nine elections I was privileged to win and the one I lost, election number five. Also noted are significant milestones along my eighteen-year pathway as mayor.

Peter Torigian:
He served as a marine in the United States Armed Forces and later worked as a letter carrier for the U.S. Post Office. Peter went on to become the mayor of Peabody, Massachusetts, serving in that capacity for 23 years, developing a strong business base whose tax revenues funded many city improvements. Peter earned an outstanding reputation statewide over the course of his mayoral tenure.

An Appreciated Thank You

A prominent achievement during my tenure as mayor was the reconstruction and redevelopment of the former "Shoe" property in downtown Beverly by Cummings Properties, spearheaded by developer Bill Cummings. The following two pages show an expression of appreciation when the Cummings Center reached completion. As you read on you will learn the history of this project, which contributed mightily to "Bringing Beverly Back From The Brink."

To Mayor Bill Scanlon —
...without whose great support and many extra effort(s) during the last 18 months this historic rebirth would never have occurred.
    Bill Cummings
    March 3, 1997

To Mayor Bill Scanlon —
— without whose great support
and many extra efforts during the
last 18 months this historic rebirth
would never have occurred.
Bill Cummings
March 3, 1997

The Early Years

Mine was a happy childhood. I was a war baby born in 1940. One of my earliest recollections is reading the newspaper on the day the war ended. The headline was printed in the largest letters that would fit on the front page. In order for mothers to be available for the war effort, a la Rosie the Riveter, children like me were sent to school a year younger than they normally would have been.

My parents were frugal, especially my father. They had lived through the Great Depression. We lived in a two-family home on a busy main street in Dorchester. MBTA buses ran back and forth every few minutes. My father was fond of saying, "The people who rent the downstairs pay for the house. That way we get free housing."

I walked to and from the local elementary school from kindergarten through grade six. When I was in the sixth grade my parents told me that next year I would attend the Boston Latin School, the oldest public school in the United States, dating back to 1635. At that time the school was just for boys. There was no discussion of alternative schools. That was that. What did I know? I did what I was told.

The daily trip to Latin School involved a bus, a train and a streetcar each way. It cost five cents in the morning and another five in the afternoon. On the first day of school students were split into groups of four. A teacher sat down with each group and said, "Look around you; one of you will graduate in six years; the other three will not make it." I didn't really believe him but it turned out to be very close to the truth when I looked at the actual numbers years later.

Latin School insisted that each of us do three hours of homework every school night, but that wasn't too bad. Every afternoon after getting off the bus we had a couple of hours to play pickup games in whatever sport was in season before supper and then do our homework. The six-year curriculum was identical for every student with two exceptions. The student had to choose between study of the Greek or German language in the tenth grade to go along with Latin, French and English, which were mandatory. I chose German. The student could also select the scientific option in grade twelve to focus on physics, chemistry and mathematics if his grades were high enough, thus avoiding a sixth year of Latin. I took the scientific option in a hurry.

Looking back, it was clear that my parents wanted to instill a strong work ethic in their children. I was the middle child with sisters on both sides. During the year in which I was born there was great concern about the spread of polio amongst youngsters who spent their hot summers in the City of Boston. That same year my father with his own two hands built a summer cottage in the Town of Marshfield about thirty miles south of Boston on the seacoast. We spent our summers there. Over the years the cottage was improved and improved by my father during weekends in the spring and the fall and I was my father's gopher on all those projects. Go for this. Go for that. Fetch this. Hold that. It wasn't all fun but it probably helped keep me out of trouble.

When I was twelve, and again at age thirteen, I picked many, many quarts of wild blueberries. My father took them to Boston and sold them with the proceeds going to my savings account. When I was fourteen and fifteen after my freshman and sophomore years in high school, I was sent to caddie camp at the Hyannisport Country Club on Cape Cod where fifty-six boys lived in seven tents, eight boys per tent sleeping in four bunk beds. The camp was located on the golf course. The season ran from late June through Labor Day and we caddied seven days a week. The caddie fee for eighteen holes was $1.35. Twice that if you carried two bags, which I did often. Each boy paid $15 per week for the world's worst food, but I don't remember anyone getting sick. Both summers I came home netting more than $100.

I fondly recall my time in Hyannisport. Many evenings we would walk to a local pier and take Red Cross swimming lessons in the ocean. To get there we had to walk by the Kennedy compound. At that time, although the Kennedys were well known, there were no guards blocking access to the area. Each time we went by the Kennedy home we would deliberately throw a football into their yard and then run onto their property to retrieve it. One day nearly fifty years later at a mayor's conference, I sat next to then U.S. Senator Ted Kennedy at lunch and I told him about our football exploits on his lawn. We shared a good laugh. The reason I was given that seat next to Kennedy was that while nearly all mayors are Democrats, I have been a life-long Independent and Kennedy wanted to be friendly with me in case he ever desired my support on some issue.

Although I loved athletics I was not able to play varsity sports at Latin School. There were 2,600 boys in the school. I was both young and very small. Even when I graduated two months after turning seventeen I was only five feet one inch tall and weighed one hundred and seventeen pounds.

As my six years at Latin School neared its end the understanding at home was that if I could get into MIT (Massachusetts Institute of Technology), I would go there. As I write these words I am only now fully realizing how programmed my life was. There was no discussion about which college to attend. The subject of living away at school never came up. My parents had decided what they thought was best for me and what did I know. Except for a fallback position with a couple of other colleges in case I was not accepted by MIT, that was that. In fact, I was too young and I was too sheltered and I had spent the last six years in all male environments.

And so in September 1957 I began my college education at MIT. Now instead of the bus, the train and the streetcar, I took the same bus and the same train followed by a long walk. I was one of many commuting students. Fortunately, I now had an old car by my second year. That was important because my family had moved to the town of Braintree. There were no buses to be had.

I mentioned earlier my folks being frugal. Tuition at Latin School had been free for Boston residents but quite steep for out-of-towners. Once I had graduated my parents moved out of the city.

I set no records as a student at MIT. I had been a better student in high school but now I enjoyed my freedom. I attended all my classes but did very little homework. I played a lot of poker at the non-resident students club and generally won pocket change. I also grew five inches and gained thirty-five pounds in my freshman year. MIT didn't pursue athletes. I was able to play four years of varsity ice hockey as a result. Our teams were nothing special.

College, the Military and Graduate School

Reserve Officer Training Corps (ROTC) was a requirement for all MIT freshman students; after that it was optional but continuance led to an easy commission as a military officer upon college graduation. I found ROTC to be exceptionally boring and I quickly gave it up as a sophomore. In those days military service was a universal requirement and frankly I looked forward to serving, but I would deal with that subject after college.

While in college I would change my major several times. First I tried Chemical Engineering, but was put off by the pungent smells of chemicals in the laboratories. I had only chosen that major because my friends had made that choice. I soon switched to Geology. I liked the subject and the chance to be outdoors often, but one day out on a field trip with several students and two PhD professors, (one from MIT and one from Berkeley California) I heard two entirely different explanations as to what the available physical evidence at an outcrop site demonstrated had happened about a million years ago.

Right then I knew I had to pursue something more definite for a field of study. So I switched to Mechanical Engineering, a truly complex subject. That didn't work out. The truth is that I was not willing at that time to work hard enough to do it justice. So I switched once again to Civil Engineering which suited me well. It would turn out many years later to be very helpful in solving Beverly's age-old flooding problems that affected thousands of residents.

As I entered my senior year, I had gone to school for seventeen consecutive years, including kindergarten. My motivation was low, but I did just enough work to graduate in the spring of 1961.

I got a job making $100 per week. My father had told me years earlier that once you earned $100 a week you had it made. That was his magic number. I worked for the Massachusetts Port Authority as a draftsman.

I knew that the military service issue would come up fast, in a matter of weeks or at most months. The Universal Draft was still in place. I had been deferred while in college. Now I knew the call from the Draft Board would be coming. I chose to pursue the Officer Candidate School (OCS) route and remarkably I had my draft physical exam and my OCS physical on two consecutive days. Shortly thereafter I entered Navy OCS in Newport, Rhode Island in February 1962 as a Seaman Apprentice.

The OCS experience was like the Charles Dickens novel, "The Tale of Two Cities," famous for the line, "It was the best of times, it was the worst of times..." I am very glad to have experienced OCS, as it was a life changing experience, but I would not want to do it again for any amount of money. Incidentally, at OCS we were paid $72.88 per month; that's right per month. The instructors tried every day to get you to tell them to go commit an unnatural act. Under my breath they succeeded but not out loud. At OCS the candidate never had a free minute. We were always busy, often doing dumb things but always busy. We had two Navy issue coats in our lockers. It often rained in Newport. When one coat got wet, we wore the other one. When that got wet we swapped one wet one for the other still wet one.

We marched everywhere we went. If our end target was one hundred feet from where we started, we often walked 1,000 yards around the block in the rain to get there. If anyone complained, he was immediately washed out.

If you washed out, and many did, the next day you would be in the chow line serving breakfast to the men who yesterday had been your classmates. It was the ultimate embarrassment for those who failed.

Among the things I learned at OCS was what a jerk I could be. Having not studied much in college I was determined to do my very best at OCS. After taking a test I would complain about getting one question out of ten wrong while some classmates hearing me would be hoping to have gotten six questions right and avoid being washed out. That didn't make me any friends. I was very self-centered.

After a while I began to catch on and for the first time in my life I started to listen and think about the other guy. An extraordinary man who many years later did much to help the City of Beverly get back on its feet was Steve Dodge. He too went through Navy OCS and shortly before his untimely death, he offered public comments similar to mine. He and I both learned to listen and to think about others at OCS.

One experience late in my days at OCS stands out. Shortly before we were to take a final written exam, a classmate still fearing washing out approached me and said that he felt sure that a problem involving latitude and longitude measured in degrees, minutes, and seconds would be on the test and asked if I could make him a template such that he could solve any problem of that sort. I was happy to help and did so.

Sure enough, the exam contained such a question. After the exam my classmate approached me blurting out the answer he had calculated. I told him that my answer was the same as his. He was ecstatic. I remember his words, "I've made it." It turned out that my template had been widely shared with other students and that gave me a very good feeling. I had learned a lot about getting along with others.

In June I was commissioned as an Ensign in the Civil Engineer Corps of the U.S. Navy, which meant I would be land based during my three years of service to follow. As an officer my salary increased to $222 per month.

After graduation I was sent to California for two months for instruction specific to Civil Engineer Corps Officers. From there I was transferred to the Naval Station in Argentia, located in the province of Newfoundland, Canada. That stand-alone site had two steam and electricity cogeneration plants as well as its own water supply and distribution system. I worked with both uniformed and civilian personnel on public services as well as cost estimating and contract administration. I also met a woman named Nancy Blair. She lived in the capitol city of St. John's and was a Registered Nurse. We dated during almost the entire year and a half I was stationed in Newfoundland. We married the day before I was to leave for my next duty station, the Naval Supply Center in Bayonne, New Jersey.

A Supply Corps Admiral was in charge of that vast facility and very surprisingly I soon found myself reporting directly to him. He was a terrific boss. We really hit it off. I had never been responsible for large sums of money. Now I was responsible for millions of dollars. I enjoyed being responsible. I was in charge of all Engineering and Public Services on the base. We did a lot of things including building a church because that is what the Admiral wanted. The work was enjoyable and exciting. My military service was fast becoming the most useful part of my education. I seriously considered making the Navy a career, but I was concerned that not all future bosses would be as inspiring as the Admiral had been. I also determined that I did not want to spend the rest of my career as an engineer.

In January of 1965, a few months before my military service would end, I visited Ben Martin, my hockey coach at MIT and told him I wanted to apply to the Harvard Business School (HBS) in pursuit of an MBA. Ben told me that another former MIT hockey player, though not one I had ever met, was working in the admissions office at HBS. So he picked up the phone and called the guy. Almost too good to be true, forty-five minutes later I was up the river in the admissions office at HBS talking face to face with a man with whom I had something in common. We were both hockey players. The discussion was frank, direct, and helpful. A prerequisite to admission would be taking the Graduate Record Exam in Business. I was told that if I scored at or above a certain number on the test, my chances of being accepted would be good. I did and was accepted. I made a couple of other applications but HBS was my goal. I am sure that a highly positive letter of recommendation from the Supply Corps Admiral did not hurt my chances. My military service ended that June.

I began my two years at HBS in September of 1965. The incoming class was divided into sections of about 95 students each who met daily in an amphitheater setting. Each night we were assigned three "cases." A case was a story, real or imaginary, about a given company with problems, often thinly disguised, which we were to analyze and be ready to discuss in terms of possible solutions the following day in front of 95 or so students and the professor.

The deal was this. There was not time to fully analyze three cases a night. That was impossible. So the approach taken was to study case one thoroughly, case two somewhat less and case three very little. The professors were determined to fail and expel five percent of the first year students and the professors got together outside class to share notes and find out whose performance was shaky. It was unusual to get called on more than once in a given hour-long class. If you faced the situation of being ill prepared for a case discussion, an often effective tactic was to make a bland non-controversial statement early in the discussion. It was unlikely that you would have to speak again during that session.

Two objectives of the professors were clear. Number one was to show everyone that often times in the real world one does not have the time to fully analyze a situation. The second objective was to show how tough and demanding the school was.

The other bogeyman was the need for each student to frequently write papers called WACS (Written Analysis of Cases) that would be corrected and graded by female college students of English who supposedly knew nothing about business. These papers were required every two weeks and would be marked up anonymously and returned to the authors and be the only written feedback HBS freshman students received until final exams were given at the end of the semester. The feedback in the form of grades on WACS from anonymous graders was incredibly difficult for many students to accept. It led to a great many cases of low morale and poor performance in class.

But for me the whole process was very rewarding. I relished all the different situations the cases allowed me to consider and analyze. I was fully engaged and worked very hard. I regularly received decent grades on my papers. A few weeks into the term I became a father for the first time as my wife and I welcomed our daughter Barbara into the world.

In the summer between my two years at HBS I worked for the United Shoe Machinery Corporation whose worldwide headquarters were located in Boston. The company was in the process of changing its name to the USM Corporation.

Until the mid 1800s all the shoes worn in the entire world had been handmade. The birth of mechanization of shoemaking began in Lynn, Massachusetts and in the 1890s five fledgling machine builders "united" to form the United Shoe Machinery Corporation and soon relocated to Beverly. That company essentially controlled the worldwide market for shoe machinery for more than half a century. Incredibly successful, the company had profited more from the mechanization of shoemaking than any other company in the world, but by the 1950s foreign competition, industry maturity, trends to casual footwear and the verdict by the United States Federal Court that USM Corporation was indeed a monopoly all joined together to attack the company.

(I will provide more about the origins of the United Shoe Machinery Corporation in later chapters.)

Thanks to my summer employment I got to know many of the key players at USM and developed good relationships. I sensed that there would be real opportunity within the company as it tried to replace lost business with acquisitions. I had several job offers at the end of my second year at HBS. USM offered me a position in the Corporate Planning Department with a starting salary of $15,000 per year. I took the job. It paid nearly three times my father's magic number of $100 per week. It seemed like a fortune at the time.

Going To Work

After less than three months on the job at the Boston headquarters I was asked to see what help I could give to a very recent acquisition, the Parker Kalon Company (PK) located in northern New Jersey. I would be the Assistant to the President of PK, a manufacturer of self-tapping screws.

USM had acquired PK just months earlier but already it was losing serious money. Not knowing how long the assignment would last, I began commuting, leaving Massachusetts at 4:00 a.m. Mondays and returning home leaving New Jersey at 5:00 p.m. Fridays. I believed it was important to be present every hour the business doors were open.

The president of PK was a very decent man, but he was badly out of place in the troubled situation that existed. He spent nearly every minute in his office. His door was open and sometimes someone ventured in but he hardly ever ventured out. There were no meetings of department heads. There was no plan.

Fortunately for me he gave me full rein. I, of course, had never run a troubled company but I was eager to try. I had no formal power but perhaps that was a blessing. I had the opportunity to work with department heads and others to get them to fully understand our status and problems and work toward finding solutions.

PK was a business with revenues of $10,000,000 per year, but already it was losing money at the rate of $1,000,000 annually. Screws may seem to be a simple product but their manufacture generally requires several different operations, and finished products varied by diameter, length, head style and thread style, by material and more. As a result, the product line contained many thousands of items.

The company lacked a useful product costing system. Pricing of products was all over the place and the price a customer paid for product often depended on which customer service representative handled a phone order. Bargaining occurred on the pricing of many orders. The entire business was wholesale. No one paid the list price. Screws were sold in thousand piece quantities. The price of a single screw was very often a fraction of a cent... hard to believe if you have purchased any screws at your local hardware store recently.

With herculean efforts from the Finance Director and the Data Processing Manager we upgraded and improved the costing system. That enabled us to stop giveaway pricing. We also improved order entry, which improved delivery lead times and helped us obtain additional orders. People placing orders often see screws as minor items that need to be available quickly. Meeting that demand helped increase business.

A point was made of making every employee aware of our status and problems, with the hint that continued losses threatened the very existence of the company and their jobs. Month after month we shared operating results with everyone. Since I was far from home I had time to work well into the evenings, setting a positive and helpful example. Most people really do want to do a good job. Slowly we began to make progress and after eighteen months improved the business to a break-even level. All that work just to break even.

The decision had recently been made at Corporate to break the entire worldwide business of USM into three groups — Machinery, Chemicals and Fasteners. PK was made part of the Fastener Group and I was recalled to Boston. Back at headquarters my efforts had been appreciated. The situation had been improved by $1,000,000 per year. The bleeding had stopped.

I had learned a lot. USM in its quest to replace lost machinery revenues had acquired a highly competitive, low margin business with no proprietary manufacturing advantage, located in the high labor cost shadow of Manhattan Island with no real plan for the future. I vowed to myself that going forward I would expend my efforts where there was opportunity to make significant profits.

I had been back at headquarters in Boston only a few months when the announcement was made that Al Snow, the Director of the Corporate Planning Department and the man who had hired me, was to be put in charge of all of USM's Canadian businesses as President of USM Ltd. headquartered in Montreal, Quebec. USM Ltd. was a much smaller version of the parent company that manufactured and marketed the products of all three groups, Machinery, Chemicals and Fasteners.

Al asked me if I would like to join him and relocate my family to Montreal. In recent years USM Ltd. had not performed well, actually losing money. A look at revenues and total employment showed that USM Ltd. had very low revenues per employee. While the shoe machinery business had been in decline, nearly all the products marketed by the company, including machinery, had attractive gross margins that should have led to profitable results.

My family and I were thrilled with the opportunity and I quickly said yes to the move. By now our family had grown to four with the addition of our son, Bill. I looked forward to playing ice hockey once again and to teaching my children to skate. Indeed, we were able to build a rink in the backyard of our new home with natural ice from Thanksgiving to St. Patrick's Day. We used the rink nearly every day.

I followed Al Snow to Montreal by three months and started work as the Vice President of Manufacturing. That was my title but Al and I had agreed that I would take a keen interest in all problems and opportunities. I began working long hard days. Al had already eliminated the company limousine and let go the company chauffeur. That sent a message to everyone. Things were going to be different.

The company had recently constructed an expensive first-class office building thus separating those functions from the rest of the business. That to my mind had been a strange decision. We were not engaged in a growth business. There was no real need to have created more space. Unfortunately the presence of the fancy new building was helping create the feeling amongst the workforce that some employees were more important than others. Analysis of those working in the new building showed that many assistants had an assistant. Here we were, losing money in an environment that was not encouraging a strong team effort.

It wasn't long before we decided to turn things around. We began to renovate a portion of the largest factory building to provide sufficient but less office space than the new building contained, and we put the new building up for sale. Simultaneously, we initiated a strong attrition policy. We combined job duties whenever possible to give some people greater responsibility and increased compensation. Some people who knew they were under-employed began to look elsewhere for jobs. We also initiated an early retirement plan that many people chose to accept.

Early retirement programs do not always make financial sense, but when the people who choose to retire do not have to be replaced, they generally make a lot of sense.

While the parent company had recently decided to operate as three separate groups, we were able at least for now to operate as one company with three product lines. Our geographic approach was cost effective. The newly formed worldwide groups would face several years with bigger things to worry about than the Canadian business. I believe I was the only person in the entire worldwide multi-billion-dollar company involved in the manufacturing and distribution of items for all three product groups. It gave me a background no one else had.

When I arrived in Montreal the company had 500 employees. Two years later after the relocation of the office workers to the factory site, we operated with a total of approximately 300 persons and we achieved that with no loss of business or inconvenience to our customers. We had instilled a strong work ethic and created an effective team effort. A positive and happy mood enveloped the company as it became quite profitable with greatly decreased expenses.

Getting the job done effectively with a much smaller workforce was the single largest contributor to profits. The reduced operating costs brought about by selling the new building were also significant, adding a six figure annual contribution to the profitability. Beyond that we made many good decisions to improve our performance. One of these in particular deserves mention.

A major part of the success of the shoe machinery business over the years all over the world was the leasing of the shoemaking machines. Upon the expiration of leases the machines returned to United would be upgraded with the latest improvements from a worldwide R&D effort and put back on lease. In Canada we engaged in both rebuilding and building new. We procured the vast majority of the needed parts from the Beverly, Massachusetts factory. USM paid significant duties to the Canadian Government in order to bring the parts across the border.

It made no sense to me that the Canadian Government would want to raise the cost to make shoes in Canada. In-depth examination of the duties showed that misclassification of parts on border crossing paperwork was the culprit and a great many parts were eligible for duty-free entry.

That saved us a lot of money going forward. On top of that our customs broker was able to reach back and obtain refunds from the Canadian Government for duties unnecessarily paid over several years. This investigation showed that sometimes it is very important to get involved in the details.

The five years I spent in Montreal were great. On the business side we repeatedly qualified for the 50 percent of salary annual maximum bonus. Colleagues in the States where operating results were much inferior were no doubt jealous.

On the human side of things nearly every company employee was bilingual, speaking both French and English. French had been my favorite language in high school and I had worked hard at it in Montreal with some success. I believe the workforce appreciated my efforts. As my time in Montreal neared the five-year mark I could hear the ice cracking. The worldwide splitting of the business into three groups had now been in effect for five years and the group presidents wanted their piece of USM Ltd. Our geographic approach, successful as it was, came under increasing pressure. I would have to choose a group and become part of it.

I felt connected to the machinery group that had been the backbone of the company. I knew many of the key players. At this time I was offered the job of Director of Operations at the massive Beverly, Massachusetts facility. It was a much bigger job than any I had held. There was no way to say no. I would be returning to my home state after a dozen years of largely being away from it.

Restructuring The Massive Beverly Operation

I was transferred to Massachusetts in the summer of 1974. I had visited the Beverly site several times but had never tried to fully comprehend it. The site was truly massive with 1,500,000 square feet of space under roof in the main complex. That is the equivalent of twenty-five football fields including end zones. The main complex had been constructed in four phases starting in 1907 and ending in 1929. They were a construction marvel of reinforced concrete when first built. An on-site cogeneration plant provided steam and electricity. There was no public electric utility in 1907.

On this site had been manufactured huge numbers of shoemaking machines starting in 1908 and continuing to the present day. The total output over time was no doubt measured in millions of machines. At the peak of business in the United States in the 1920s, 1930s and 1940s more than 100,000 such machines were making shoes every business day across the country in customers' factories, and people all across the USA were spending their days wearing out those shoes. What could be better for business? Each machine was on lease from USM. One thousand roadmen, as they were called, all employees of USM, provided free service to these machines. The service was free, but the repair parts were anything but free.

USM had been a master at fully exploiting the so-called unit charge. To allow easy financial entry into shoemaking, customers were charged only a modest rental fee for each month of service but every time a machine performed an operation such as attaching a heel or a sole to a shoe a charge of a penny or two was run up. Vital machines had counters to collect usage information. Customers were happy to pay the unit charge when they had production orders to build shoes.

The facility in Beverly was known locally as "The Shoe" which gave rise to the impression that shoes were made there. That was not the case.

The company made the machines that made the shoes but never a pair of shoes — perhaps a left or a right shoe, but not a pair. USM did not want its customers to think for a moment that it was in competition with them.

"The Shoe" had been the source of lifetime employment for three generations of employees. A huge percentage of employees were members of the Quarter Century Club signaling at least twenty-five years of employment.

When I first arrived I made it a point to spend a lot of time in the factory visiting every corner of every floor, meeting as many people as possible. It took about four hours to walk through all the spaces in the main complex. I also established a wide "open door" policy. Anyone could stop by my office at any time, no appointment needed.

To the best of my knowledge my predecessors had all been aristocrats. I was a blue collar kid from Dorchester. I wanted to relate to the people. I made it a point to work long hours. If you are going to expect others to work long and hard I believe you have to set an example and work long and hard yourself.

I knew the factory was losing money and I knew I had been sent to Beverly to remedy that, but I wanted to fully understand the nature of the problems before making any key decisions.

I was aware that domestic shoe production was declining quickly as imported shoes gained market share. USM's secret of success over many years had been to spend heavily on R&D, patent its innovations all over the world, enforce the patents vigorously and lease its equipment rather than sell the machines. When leases expired USM would upgrade the returned equipment with the latest developments and cycle the machines back into customers' factories on new leases. At its peak USM had more than forty individual companies in countries throughout the world. It was a truly international business.

That's how it had been, but those days were gone forever. After 50 plus years of successful R&D the industry was largely mature and opportunities to improve productivity through R&D were few and far between. Much worse, nearly all the patents had expired and very real competition from Italian and Asian shoe machinery manufacturers now existed. These competitors were both lean and nimble with good equipment and low prices.

On top of all that, in the late 1950s the United States Government had successfully prosecuted the United Shoe Machinery Corporation for being a monopoly and forced the divestiture of a significant part of the company here in the United States. It also wreaked havoc on the unit charge approach and forced the company to shift from leasing to outright sales of equipment in many cases.

On my walks through the factory I couldn't help but notice large quantities of returned shoemaking machines seemingly everywhere. In addition, I learned that two large offsite buildings had been rented by USM and that they too were full of returned shoemaking machines. It was clear to me that these returned machines would never again be used to make shoes.

The business plan that had worked so well for so long was no longer relevant. We had to face the fact that the business had changed markedly. The returned machines must go to the foundry to be melted down. The horrible truth was that management had been unable to face the fact that significant restructuring would be required in the face of a greatly reduced business or the result would be bankruptcy.

That was not the only problem. As the proprietary workload needed to feed the 4,000 man-hour-per-day production capability dwindled, it was human nature to try to backfill the workload by seeking outside contract work.

The factory capabilities were broadly based and the facility had an excellent reputation for high quality work. Outside work is not a bad thing per se and can make good sense in modest amounts to backfill a lull in orders or to fill out the workload of highly specialized equipment, but it simply does not provide sufficient gross margins.

The factory found itself doing work for IBM, for Xerox and for a half dozen of America's largest machinery builders. Now the majority of the machinery work in the factory was being done for outsiders and the numbers just didn't add up.

I am a very direct person, sometimes blunt. It seems I do my best work when things are troubled. My approach is to be absolutely straightforward with everyone. I knew the workforce was intelligent. I believed they could take the truth. Essex County, which includes Beverly, had the highest per capita income of any county in the United States in the late

1930s, not primarily because of the very rich but because of companies like United Shoe Machinery Corporation and others that generated thousands of good jobs. Other major contributors to that ranking were General Electric, Western Electric and Sylvania.

Throughout the entire process, I was up front with the facts. There is an old saying that if you tell the truth you don't have to remember what you said yesterday. Many, many people I have dealt with do not subscribe to this approach and if you go straight ahead with them you fool them every time.

Sometimes being blunt works well. Sometimes it doesn't. It works best when things are really a mess and that is why I have always done my best work when things were at their worst.

Fortunately, very fortunately, the factory was unionized. This statement will likely shock some readers, but let me explain. Factory workers were members of a fiercely independent United Electrical Workers local. My task was to explain to a half dozen key Union officials what I thought had to be done and if we could reach agreement on that, they in turn would explain things to their hundreds of members. There is no way I could ever have reached their membership directly. I would have been shouted down.

There were also hundreds of salaried workers. Again, fortunately the department heads that supervised these people were competent and willing to face reality. We had to shrink the organization significantly and we had to cut back markedly on outside contract work. Many, many jobs would be lost, but our choice was to lose some in order to save others or lose them all and close the doors.

We called it the "Lifeboat Theory" for obvious reasons. Far from hiding what had to be done we solicited thoughts and suggestions that might help us through perilous times.

And so the restructuring process began. We terminated the leases on buildings providing off-site machinery storage. We began melting down excess returned machines in the Foundry. We laid out a plan to consolidate machine tools at one end of the plant. We posted drawings of the proposed layout and invited suggestions and comment. We freed up 150,000 square feet of space on the factory floor and leased it to the local vocational technical high school. We returned a large boring mill being used for outside contract work to its manufacturer, thus eliminating a $360,000 annual lease payment. And we began a series of what would be four large layoffs over an eighteen-month period, all occurring on Fridays. The layoff process necessarily had to be done in steps, each time allowing the dust to settle while ensuring that internal changes were not affecting our customers adversely.

Our inventory contained approximately 100,000 shoe machinery part numbers. Our goal was to ship at least 90% of all repair parts orders on the same day the order was received. We needed every employee to work diligently and effectively, despite the difficult situation which became more dire with each layoff. Everyone in the facility, both union and salaried, knew what was happening and wondered if he or she would be next.

As the layoffs continued I had doctors calling me telling me I was killing people and they were probably correct. People who had known no other job actually felt ashamed about losing their job. As I will explain later, it is not something persons can fully understand until it happens to them.

The truth is we didn't know just where the bottom would be found. To some extent it was by trial and error. We had to keep shrinking the organization while at the same time keeping it functional until we had eliminated the factory's severe financial loss.

There was one aspect of the cutbacks that was self-correcting. Most chip cutting jobs had been time studied and many machinists worked on an incentive basis. When the workload shrank machinists with significant seniority would insist that others with less seniority be laid off so that the more senior machinists could continue to receive full incentive pay that sometimes reached 1.8 of the standard. If meeting standard meant wages of $200 per week, performance at 1.8 of standard would mean 80% more or $360 per week. In this respect the incentive system self-policed employment levels.

About a year into the eighteen-month process, I was called into the office of my boss to discuss the factory loss of about $2,000,000 annually. The Finance Director was also present. The boss asked me when the factory loss would disappear. I said that we would reach break-even in six months. He then asked the Finance Director the same question and his response was that the loss was not going away despite all the cutbacks. The boss then said to the Finance Director, "If we give Corporate your answer they will fire all of us now. If we go with Bill's answer, we have six months to fix things, so we will go with Bill's answer."

As the process of cutting back continued, one particularly hard hit group was the foremen. Men who had stood out as loyal, learned and effective employees and who had been rewarded with promotions to salaried foremen positions were among the most affected with two out of every three losing their jobs. I remember asking myself, do these people hate me? Do they see me as the problem? I am sure there was some of that. I will never know how much.

During the restructuring process I had heavy involvement with local newspapers, both the Beverly Times and the Salem News. USM was still the largest employer in the City of Beverly despite the cutbacks. To their credit, reporters were willing to listen to me as I outlined our problems and explained that we had to eliminate some jobs to save others or we would eventually lose all the jobs. The newspapers were fair throughout the ordeal.

In early 1976 the last of the four layoffs occurred. I knew quite well many of the people let go that day and I felt terrible. To be honest I admit that I literally tried hard that evening to drown my sorrows, but my efforts did not help one bit. It was a rough night. One I will never forget.

When the dust settled the number of employees who still had a job was 710, as close as one can get to one-half of the 1,421 which had existed eighteen months earlier when I had arrived in Beverly.

The factory loss was gone. Fortunately my prediction had proven correct. In fact, we were entering a period of employment stability that would last for the next ten years. There was also good news in the form of new factory workload. Before describing that I want to make mention of my interaction with the union both during the layoff period and after.

The relationship with the union was founded on trust and honesty. We had been straight with one another. After one set of contract negotiations was complete and we were about to go public, the Chief Steward, Harry Ball, told me, "Look, we have a deal, but when we go public you are going to take some shots. So stay cool." He was right. I took some shots, but we had a deal.

Harry Ball was a good man. The city-owned baseball field located about 1,000 yards from my home bears his name. I remember the size of his fist, at least twice the size of mine, which I suspect at some point in the past had been called into action with some union member who had difficulty understanding what was best for him. When the ball field was dedicated in Harry's name I remember writing a newspaper article describing Harry Ball as that "gruff, gentle giant."

On another occasion we had completed wage negotiations with the union that called for a raise for everyone except foundry workers who represented a small percentage of the total workforce. The foundry had become almost solely dependent on outside work because modern machinery rarely involved castings. The foundry was losing money.

When the proposal was presented to the union membership, a union member suggested that all those getting a raise take a little bit less than the agreement called for and that those savings be applied to the foundry workers so that in the end all the employees would be treated exactly the same way and that the company's total cost would be identical to what had been earlier agreed to. This proposal demonstrated caring amongst the workers and I quickly agreed to it.

The good news I alluded to earlier came in two parts. The first, the last great advancement in shoemaking from the R&D laboratory in Beverly reached the market in the form of computer controlled automatic stitching machines. Made in Beverly, these machines were a huge hit in the cowboy boot industry for decorative stitching and around the world for the assembly of shoe parts.

The second piece of good news was the Beverly production of electronic component insertion machinery under the Dyna Pert name. These close tolerance machines operated at high speeds inserting axial lead components in printed circuit boards. Their production generated significant factory work hours.

Harry Ball
Harry was an imposing figure, a large man with massive fists. At the same time he was very intelligent, thoughtful and reacted very well to the truth no matter how painful it was. Despite his gruff exterior, a nicer man I never met. As the Chief Steward of the United Electrical Workers Union at the "Shoe," Harry was a voice of reason who helped add ten years to the life of the company.

With the factory loss gone I was promoted to be in charge of the entire U.S. business including marketing, R&D and P&L responsibility. In this new role I spent a lot of time meeting major United States customers. As the reader knows, USM had historically relied on the leasing of equipment but the guilty monopoly verdict had shifted the emphasis to the sale of machinery. Never, not even once, had a customer been asked to place a down payment or deposit prior to a machinery installation in the customer's factory.

At this time we received an inquiry from a major customer for 50 computer stitching machines costing $50,000 each. As I pondered this prospect and visited the customer's factory in Florida, something told me that we had to request a deposit of size before manufacturing the machines. That thinking was revolutionary in view of our history but I stuck to it.

If we were to have built all that inventory and their order failed to materialize, I would have been in very hot water because of the large amount of money tied up in the major inventory build. My thinking was that if the customer really wants 50 machines, why would he mind making a deposit? I could not think of a good reason so I stuck to my position. With that, the interest on the customer's part waned and eventually disappeared. It turned out to be a good decision on my part.

While 1976 finally brought stability to operations at Beverly, at the corporate level things were not good. USM had made a number of acquisitions but most of them did not fare well. The company lacked skill in both acquiring and then in managing the acquisitions. By this time the company's stock, which was listed on the New York exchange, was not doing well. Several suitors were actively trying to take over the company and the company was not in a good position to fend them off. The Emhart Corporation of Farmington, Connecticut emerged as the victor. For me that was not bad news. The Emhart people, while not possessed of great humor, were very direct and if you performed well, you were rewarded well.

The year 1976 also saw my wife Nancy and I reach the decision to divorce. We both decided that would be best for everyone. The process was amicable.

Worldwide Responsibility

In 1977 I took part in a hard look at the way the Shoe Machinery Group was organized. The companies around the world marketing and servicing shoe machinery operated largely independently and currently numbered nearly two dozen. Three distinct locations performed significant R&D and also had sizable manufacturing facilities. They were: Beverly, Massachusetts; Leicester, England; and Rodelheim, Germany.

The objective of reorganization was to be able to decide centrally where to spend R&D dollars, where to manufacture a given machine, how much inventory to build, how to bring a new machine to market and the like.

The process of making shoes is inherently labor intensive, even with the best of production equipment. People anywhere can be taught to make shoes. Thus the production of shoes invariably shifts to low labor cost countries. We needed a nimble and knowledgeable group of marketing personnel who would readily travel anywhere in the world to pursue business opportunities. To meet that need a group was established known as the Footwear Industry Organization (FIO) made up of Americans, English, French and Germans, all experts in their shoemaking disciplines, who would add these new duties to their existing obligations in their home countries. I was put in charge of the FIO with a Frenchman as the Worldwide Director of Marketing. It was a truly international organization with highly competent staff.

The amount of travel to do the job was very extensive. We met every ninety days at one of the R&D locations to review project status, make hard decisions, review worldwide forecasting, make inventory build decisions and coordinate our strategy on a worldwide basis. For the next five years I spent more than 100 nights per year sleeping in foreign hotel rooms. My son thought I worked for the CIA! I carried two passports because sometimes one had to be tied up while pursuing a visa to enter a country. It was a terrific geography lesson. They were great years. The staff was hardworking and talented. We had a very effective team.

During this entire period I kept my office in Beverly but was often away. The FIO concept worked well. In 1982 two things of importance occurred. On the personal side of things, I married Louise LeBlanc, a lady born in Canada who came to the United States as a young woman and became a naturalized citizen. Fluently bilingual, she worked as an executive secretary. Louise and I had dated for several years. We enjoy speaking to each other in French. Looking back as I write these words, marrying Louise was the best thing that ever happened to me. She was also a big hit with my children who were teenagers at that time.

The other item of import was my promotion to the position of President of the Shoe Machinery Group with companies in over twenty countries, at least one on every continent except Antarctica.

The new job gave me line authority over all the Shoe Machinery companies around the world. Naturally the emphasis on heavy international travel continued. I brought experience to the job and emphasis on cost effective management in units both large and small as evidenced in the United States and Canada. We were in a highly competitive world. We continued the work of the FIO on forecasting and inventory building and continued the practice of R&D reviews four times per year. We also emphasized the need for cost control in every unit mirroring the success in North America. I reviewed every country's annual budget personally. By 1986 we had trimmed our sails effectively.

The year 1986 demonstrated the success of our work. Operating results were extremely good as the year's end approached. We were on our way to the best results in my nearly twenty years with the company.

The Sudden End

In late December of 1986 I arrived at the office in Beverly on a Monday morning and learned to my astonishment that the entire shoe machinery business had been sold by the parent company Emhart to a newly formed company in England. I also learned that I would be out of a job by the end of the month.

There is no question I was shocked by the sale and by the utter coldness of the way my termination was handled. There was no discussion with senior corporate management. It took a bit of time to digest things.

Over the next few days it became clear that the intention of the new owners was to remove all shoe machinery related functions from the Beverly site. The Dyna Pert business would also be moved leaving the massive Beverly site virtually empty, lying idle in the heart of the city. The newspapers covered the entire story in depth including the fact that I would be let go. At least what was happening would not be blamed on me.

As I reflected on my being caught so totally off guard by what had happened, I now had the answer to two puzzling events. Two months earlier in October I had been called down to headquarters in Connecticut to meet with the new Chief Executive Officer of Emhart, Mr. Peter Scott.

In the course of an amicable discussion he asked me if the shoe machinery business could grow 10-12% per year. I said no but added that I thought 6-8% was possible. I didn't think any more about that conversation but it was now clear that he had grander ideas. Around that same time in October a corporate official had suggested to me that I consider selling the leased machinery account. I had reacted strongly and negatively to that suggestion which would sacrifice the long term for the short term. I don't think that way. Now in retrospect I think I was being given a hint.

Soon we had the final results for 1986. The shoe machinery group had revenues of $150 million, pretax operating profit of $20 million and a return on the money tied up in the business of 29%. These were truly remarkable numbers.

I learned that I would receive the maximum bonus of 50% of salary for meeting all my goals and six months of severance for my years of service, in all a year's pay.

I learned that Emhart had received a good price of well over $100 million for the business and that the entire sum would be invested in a software startup company. Jumping forward for a moment, eighteen months later the software company was bankrupt and every dime from the sale of the shoe machinery business was gone.

The new owners of the shoe machinery business had been financed by venture capitalists. They would soon want to start getting their money back. Emhart had been paid in cash. To me it was patently obvious that the new owners would try to make further significant reductions in the workforce. That would not be possible. We had closely trimmed the workforce already. We were experts at that.

Everything has its limits. Now instead of cutting fat, muscle and bone were being cut. The business was soon in a death spiral and the more they cut the more the business around the world would be hurt. Within five years the entire business would be gone, totally gone. It was a sad ending to what had once been an incredible success story and as recently as 1986 had performed so very well.

One last comment on unsuccessful ventures. In 1989 Emhart Corporation was forced to merge with the much smaller Black & Decker Corporation located in Maryland. When that occurred 90% of Emhart's corporate staff in Connecticut was laid off. I wasn't surprised.

A Change In Lifestyle

The next several months provided time to think about the future. I had worked hard for nearly twenty years. During that time, when traveling abroad we flew Saturday to arrive Sunday to work Monday. When at home, Saturdays often meant a day in the office to catch up without any interruptions.

I interviewed with several large companies but my heart wasn't in it. Everything about the corporate world quickly became déjà vu. I had had it with big companies. By my standards I had made a lot of money, certainly "umpteen" times the $100 per week my Dad had talked about back in the 1950s. Now $100 might buy a good meal for two. I had also invested well.

After considerable discussion Louise and I decided to do two things. We would build a new home together; I would act as the general contractor, taking advantage of my civil engineering background. Simultaneously I started a consulting business aiding small troubled businesses.

We began the process of looking for a site for our new home as I began to seek clients. The house we had been living in was on an increasingly busy street. We found a site in Beverly on a newly developed street. The price of the land was more than what the house we would vacate had cost us, but we were excited about the site and bought the land.

I soon had several consulting clients. One client worth mention is a niche manufacturing company in southern New Hampshire. Souhegan Wood Products was family owned and had developed proprietary machinery to produce industrial products featuring the recycling of waste wood combined with appropriate resins, formed at high temperatures and pressures. These products were used extensively for the winding of conveyor belting. The company had an innate advantage with low material costs; i.e., ground waste wood, whereas competitors fashioned products from valuable lumber.

Despite the raw material advantage, the manufacturing process involved excessive handling of the products which translated into high costs and low margins. The company was in the process of changing management to a new family generation. The key individual, Randy Dunn, held a college degree in English but was extremely knowledgeable of physics, chemistry, engineering and related sciences.

I thought the future could be bright. Automation could be introduced to the manufacturing process. Other products could be developed. I spent considerable time working with Randy. Some months into the assignment a fire broke out in the plant causing extensive damage. Under-insured, the company was starved for cash and near bankruptcy. I took a chance and invested in the company, providing needed cash while taking an equity position. I worked closely with the company for a number of years. It took time but Souhegan Wood Products became quite successful. I still have a connection to it more than 30 years later as it continues to prosper.

Dialing back to the building of our new home, the process went well. We felled the trees and cleared the land. We participated extensively on work that didn't show. Each weekend we cleaned up the site so that workers could get off to a good start on Monday morning. The house was to be set back a long distance from the road.

The landscape was full of igneous outcrop, better known as granite. Extensive blasting was required. The process took the better part of a year but it was fun and it turned out well. We ended up with a very good result for a very reasonable investment. They say building a home together is the true test of a marriage, which worked very well in our case. The next few years went by quietly. I was my own boss. Life was different but it was good. I had some interesting clients and assignments. By the time 1992 arrived the City of Beverly was being bashed in the newspapers every day. There was no love lost by either the Beverly Times or the Salem News for Jack Monahan, the five-term mayor of Beverly.

The papers had endorsed other candidates in previous elections but Monahan had been able to paint his opponents as weak. At the same time the Beverly School Committee and City Council were at odds and "For Sale" signs were prevalent on homes throughout the city. I couldn't help but notice that housing prices were very low and I wondered whether the value of my newly built home might be less than the cost to erect it. That troubled me because I believed I had saved a considerable sum by being the general contractor and the end product was quite good.

My Entry Into Politics

During 1992 it was my wife Louise who first suggested I run for mayor. At first I gave it no thought. After all, I had only been in City Hall three times in my life. I had never attended a City Council meeting, but she repeated her suggestion. In the course of my consulting work I had developed a relationship with Salvi Modugno, a successful businessman and lifelong Beverly resident who had once run for the Board of Aldermen, predecessor to the City Council. He too encouraged me to run. I started to think about it. I didn't know if I could get elected but was confident in my ability to do the job. I was also aware that most city revenues are essentially guaranteed. The majority come from real estate taxes. Overdue taxes grow at usurious rates of interest, or better said, very fast. On top of that, unlike a business that has to make a profit, a city or town only has to break even.

As I talked with people about running for office, some discouraged me, saying that nobody knew me. Yet I knew from the events of nearly twenty years earlier that people in many families knew me... the question was, did they hate me? I decided that most of them would think I had just been doing my job. After all, I too had been laid off before the giant plant was emptied and turned into a massive eyesore.

I began to think seriously about becoming a candidate for mayor. I arranged a meeting with a local attorney, Tom Alexander, a go-to guy for business and development projects in Beverly. Tom had served as City Solicitor to Mayor Monahan and had resigned in disgust over some of the mayor's decisions.

> **Salvi Modugno**
> An elderly man when I met him and an established small businessman, he grew up in Beverly and attended the McKay Elementary School. He really knew his way around local politics and was one of the first people who encouraged me to run for mayor. His persistence was a major factor in my decision making.

Tom said he thought I had a chance of winning provided that I work my tail off every day of the campaign. That same day both local papers ran a story stating that Mayor Monahan had insulted Mayor Torigian of Peabody in front of a large crowd at a public event. That did it for me. He was a bully and had survived five terms by browbeating his political opposition. Someone had to stand up to him and I decided that I was that someone. I declared my candidacy immediately. That started an eight-month marathon.

We held meetings of volunteers at our home. The response was terrific. We often had about forty people at a time. I received a lot of advice, some of it quite worthwhile. One takeaway was the need to show the voting public that I really wanted the job. The easiest way to make that point was to campaign some part of every day. Knocking on doors of people on busy streets was very helpful. Even more helpful was holding evening coffees in people's living rooms with twenty or so voters present. Soon we were doing an average of four coffee chats per week.

People were gracious. The number of volunteers grew. The newspapers wanted change. That helped. There was an article in the papers nearly every day beating on the current mayor. My business background did make raising campaign funds easier. Many people wanted the city to be run more like a business.

We raised enough money to do a citywide mailing, emphasizing "Energy, Experience, and Education." While there were five declared candidates for the position, the early favorite was Bill Gelwick, a sitting City Councilor who had worked for General Electric as an accountant.

Tom Alexander
Tom grew up in Beverly, starred on the Beverly High School football team and later played for Brown University. He became a lawyer and was the "go-to" guy on most major projects in Beverly over four decades. He was, and is, the man with his ear to the ground as to what's happening in Beverly. He served as City Solicitor for a time under Mayor Monahan but resigned over decisions he could not condone. Tom is the one who introduced Bill Cummings and myself to one another.

Political lawn signs were typically installed thirty days before the primary. When that opportunity arrived volunteers built frames to accommodate the placards while Louise and I stapled many of them onto the frames. The sheer number of signs for candidate Gelwick that suddenly appeared overnight was very impressive. We had a large number of signs but nowhere near what Gelwick had. One observer reminded me that signs don't vote and that our number of signs was enough for us to be taken seriously.

In my view, people have very busy lives and little time for local politics unless things get really bad and in Beverly things had gotten really bad. Thus, people made time to get involved in the upcoming election. The energy level of people volunteering in a first-time campaign is incredible and a delight to take part in.

One night shortly before the September primary, which would shrink the field to two for the runoff in November, a televised debate was held at the Commodore Restaurant with all five candidates present. When my turn to make closing remarks came, I focused on how much housing prices had been driven down by the problems facing the city and said, "Jack Monahan has destroyed the equity in your home as surely as if he were a thief in the night robbing your possessions." I didn't realize at that time how well it resonated but indeed it did.

Shortly thereafter on primary night, all the candidates and many supporters were gathered together at the Union Club on Cabot Street. I was hoping to survive the primary. As the returns came in we were very pleasantly surprised to top the ticket with Bill Gelwick second. Mayor Monahan was a distant third. Delighted to have finally ousted Monahan, the Gelwick supporters played the song "Hit the Road Jack" over and over, at least a dozen times.

I couldn't believe my ears. Surely the Monahan voters were not going to vote for Gelwick in the final election. I kept a low profile for the next several weeks and dialed up my efforts in the last weeks before the November vote. To my delight we carried every precinct in the city with 62% of the vote. We received five out of every eight votes. The nine-member City Council saw six new members and only three incumbents reelected.

After the election victory and a few days off to celebrate, I began the process of making frequent visits to state officials in Boston apologizing to all who would listen for the poor behavior of the departing mayor over the past several years. I would need their help to regain Beverly's eligibility for various state programs and grants. On election night Governor Bill Weld had congratulated me and I took that as a good sign.

I would not be sworn into office for another six weeks but already the job had my full attention. I paid several visits to Mayor Monahan to obtain needed documents. He was gracious but each time he repeated the same mantra, "Bill, the city is broke; all the cities are broke. It is hopeless. Remember to take the summers off."

It rang in my head that this man who spent little time in his office, as witnessed by his car being regularly absent from his parking space at City Hall, had created a terrible example for city workers. As I have said before, I believe that if you expect people to work long and hard, you had better work long and hard yourself. I intended to do just that.

A large cast of people reported directly to the mayor, far too many to make sense but that would be a task for another day. I would make only one change. Attorney Ben Eisenstadt had served as City Solicitor by means of a series of temporary mayoral appointments brought on by the City Council's refusal to confirm his appointment. I of course refused to reappoint him.

I planned to retain all the others at the outset and I informed each of them one by one of my intent well before my being sworn in. I wanted to give them the chance to show that they could perform well.

I was about to officially begin the process of "Bringing Beverly Back From the Brink." I took a mental picture of what I saw. We had no money. Indeed, until we paid off a huge obligation of $8,000,000 we would have no money. The massive "Shoe" property was essentially empty. It had lain fallow since 1987 when the business had been sold. Weeds had grown tall in the parking lots. Broken windows were abundant especially along the side facing the railroad tracks where an inexhaustible supply of rocks in the form of ballast was available. The place was a giant eyesore in the heart of the city.

"For Sale" signs on houses were everywhere; housing prices had dropped markedly. The heart of the problem lay with the public schools. The School Committee and City Council had been actively at war with one another to no avail. Families moving from out of town to the North Shore saw the education of their children as a primary goal and they did not like what they saw of the Beverly schools. Thus, they relocated to neighboring cities and towns and Beverly housing prices sagged.

I knew that Mayor Monahan's mental state had been to think of Beverly as a bedroom community akin to the nearby towns of Hamilton and Wenham. I learned from talking with people that Monahan had not only discouraged development in Beverly, but that he did so in a particularly damaging manner.

When a project was first suggested he would often act in a positive way in sessions with consultants representing developers who themselves would lie low until they received encouraging feedback. Then when an initiative started to really take shape Monahan would turn negative, embarrassing the consultants and making furious both the consultants and the principals who had been misled. This behavior caused the participants to vow to avoid projects in Beverly in the future.

Beverly had and still has its share of low income citizens. It needs a solid business base to provide needed income. A quick look at the neighboring City of Peabody and the Town of Danvers showed that Peabody received 40% of its property tax revenues from business while Danvers derived 35%. Beverly trailed with 21%. Only 5 parts of that 21 came from industry, the remaining 16 parts from commercial enterprises.

Businesses not only generate more in real estate taxes than residential properties, they demand less in the way of services. Unlike residences they put no pressure on the public school systems that account for more than 50% of the annual budget of nearly every municipality. Every city and town in Massachusetts operates under the law known as Proposition 2-1/2 which limits the annual property tax overall increase on existing properties to not more than 2-1/2% above the previous year. That is the law. There are no exceptions.

Here was Beverly, badly in need of investment in its entire infrastructure that had been shortchanged for years. Its school buildings were old and run down. Significant flooding of many homes occurred every time it rained. On top of that, Beverly faced overcoming a large deficit before we could begin to fund the future.

How would we do that? Appropriate new growth, the transition of building permits into construction and then into new real estate taxes would be a major contributor. The target would be at least $1,000,000 in new growth each year.

It would take a year or two to get going but history shows we were successful. That growth would be enjoyed without adding a single acre to the land currently zoned for business. We might change a site from industrial to commercial or vice versa but we would not add one acre. We wanted to be able to suggest locations within the city that would attract people wanting to bring new businesses to Beverly.

Aside from appropriate new growth, major emphasis would be on operating more cost effectively. This approach of getting more "bang for our buck" would take many forms. It would mean watching every penny; being involved in every hire; combining jobs where possible when vacancies occurred. It would include action to ensure competition among project bidders in order to eliminate the prospect of "sweetheart" contract awards in situations where only one vendor would make a relevant proposal. I didn't know it yet, but getting people who were dead off the list of people for whom monthly health insurance payments were being made by the city to Blue Cross would turn out to yield significant savings. Those are but a few examples.

On inauguration day I appointed Marshall Handly to be the City Solicitor. After the swearing in and a brief luncheon, I held my first staff meeting with all the department heads. Shortly before the meeting was to start, Police Chief John Finnegan approached me and offered to have a police officer pick me up each morning at home and drive me to the office. I couldn't say "no" fast enough. We would have none of that. I was annoyed with the suggestion.

Marshall Handly
A young attorney who got to see much of the world early in life.
Eager, energetic, well spoken and hard working, he brought vitality to the office. After his selection as City Solicitor, his wife, Carla Cox, also a practicing attorney, commented, "You get two of us for the price of one." Her opinions were often helpful.

I began the practice of having weekly meetings of all department heads. At the end of each meeting we would go around the table with each person describing his or her most important current activity. The first person to speak was chosen randomly but I always went last. I wanted each of these people to be aware of what their colleagues were doing. Most of my contact with department heads was face to face with me often meeting them at their workplace. I almost never wrote to any of them. Face to face or by phone was my style of contact.

Almost immediately the state convened a Review Board to determine the number of years the city would be allowed to fund the deficit by generating favorable end-of-year variances sufficient to cumulatively match the full amount of the deficit of over $8,000,000. Leslie Kirwan, the very same lady who had been "savaged" by former Mayor Monahan, chaired the Review Board. Leslie went on to become the Secretary of Administration and Finance to the governor. The Secretariat was the most powerful of all the state cabinet positions. Beverly was given four years to overcome the deficit. We would do it in under three. As the first term began the level of cooperation from everyone was terrific. The city was in deep trouble and everyone knew it. The department heads were happy to have their jobs and wanted to show they could perform well. The School Committee and City Council members wanted to work together. There was no room for politics. We had a common goal; to get Beverly back on its feet. People who in better times would often disagree with one another now pulled together. I had seen this phenomenon before in the industrial turnaround situations I had faced. It was very encouraging.

My First Years In Office

A veteran mayor once told me that if people know they can access you easily they would not do so frivolously. I took that to heart. We opened the mayor's office door to everyone and I met with people on a walk-in basis as much as possible. If I could not see that person immediately, we scheduled a meeting in the very near future.

As a result of the November election both the City Council and the School Committee had multiple new members. I was now a member of the School Committee, although not the Chair, which suited me fine. I had plenty to do. I chose to attend nearly all the City Council meetings and did so for most of my entire time in office. I did that for two reasons. One was to hasten the feedback between councilors and myself. The other was that I found over time that City Councilors were much more careful what they said in front of the TV cameras when I was in the room than they were when I was not present.

Almost immediately, and to my complete surprise, I found that departing Mayor Monahan and the citizen volunteer Golf and Tennis Commission had awarded a five-year contract extension to the current golf course operator, Friel Company, during the week between Christmas and New Years. That was a severe setback because it extended Friel's current "sweetheart" deal well into the future. My hands were tied for five years during which the city would receive only "chump change" from the golf course.

Very shortly I discovered that the finance director and the prior mayor had deliberately underfunded the sewer account from which the South Essex Sewage District (SESD) was paid by $600,000 in order to present a balanced budget for the current fiscal year. I also learned that SESD charges for the fiscal year to begin July 1, 1994 would increase by $1,000,000. To cover all these costs it was necessary to raise the sewer rate by 58% to $3.56 per 100 cubic feet of effluent. The City Council quickly and unanimously approved the order for the increase. Even with that change that put Beverly in line with neighboring communities, the combined water and sewer rate was less than one cent for each gallon used by a resident and then put down the drain. Amazing, but true.

Discovery of the phony budget with $600,000 deliberately underfunded by the Finance Director proved that he would have to be removed at the appropriate time, but I had no intention of firing him until I had learned everything he knew. That would take time.

The finance director of course knew that I knew what he had done. I told him that I would personally build the budget for the upcoming fiscal year to begin July 1, 1994, leaving him out of the process entirely. I would work directly with the department heads. That would allow me to learn more about each of them and their departments. I did make contact with the finance director almost every day usually by dropping by his office totally unexpectedly. I wanted to get a handle on all his activities. I wanted to know everything I could about everything financial.

Of course, we had no money. Indeed, we had a huge deficit. What we did have was time and talent. Many years of inattention to our infrastructure had gone by. Our elementary schools were in very poor physical condition. Very shortly the School Committee and the City Council jointly established a group consisting of several members from each body as well as a number of private citizens to study the status of our elementary schools and make recommendations. The group held evening meetings open to the public that were very well attended with several hundred people often present. I attended every one of those meetings.

There were eight elementary schools in Beverly at the time. It was no secret that Beverly had very little in the way of visible minorities. It was very "whitish," but it did have its share of poverty. Twenty percent of Beverly's public school students were enrolled in the Federal Free and Reduced Lunch Program, a poverty indicator which often points to single parent families or parents whose own limited education impacted the extent to which they could help their children with their studies at home.

In the course of discussion two people in particular, Nancy Levin of the School Committee and Tom Scully, Beverly's Public Library Director, brought to light the makeup of the student population on the Free and Reduced Lunch Program in each of the elementary schools. Several of the schools had no students enrolled in the program. Others had a few.

The focus shifted to the two downtown schools, Washington Beadle and Abraham Edwards that had over 75% and over 50% respectively of their students in the Free and Reduced Lunch Program. That translated into more than three out of every four children in the Beadle School and more than two out of every four in the Edwards. The teachers in those two schools faced an impossible situation. They had too many children needing help to learn to read well. The teachers were overwhelmed.

The numbers were startling and they demonstrated clearly that all our elementary schools did not offer children equal educational opportunities. Change was essential. Yet as these discrepancies were uncovered and discussed more than a few people in the audience were quite content with the existing situation. They were happy with their personal situations and some rather prickly discussion followed. After minutes of rancor, something I will never forget happened. Several young women who were obviously pregnant spoke up eloquently insisting that the current districting policy was unfair and unacceptable. They were unstoppable and they were right. Their voices carried the day. It was clear to me that we needed to create an environment in Beverly in which all parents would be pleased to have their children attend any one of the schools because all were equally desirable.

As we investigated we found that there was no common curriculum across our elementary schools. That too would need to change.

From the meetings and much debate came a plan. We would develop a common curriculum, and we would ensure that no school had less than 15% or no more than 25% of its students on Free and Reduced Lunch. We would plan to close three schools while building one new school and upgrade and enlarge the other five. Washington Beadle and Abraham Edwards would be closed. We would first build one new school. Of course, all of this was just a plan. We had no money. History would show it was a good plan. It was late 1995 when the City Council fully approved the plan in its entirety.

It would take until the year 2003 to fully implement our school plan. More Beverly children learned to read well. Standardized testing proved that out. Our testing scores improved markedly. For me it was perhaps the most important decision I participated in during my entire time in office because it affected so many young lives in a positive way.

Shifting gears, "The Shoe" property south of Route 62 was largely vacant land. It would be sold and developed separately from the main parcel. The highest and best use of the site had been analyzed repeatedly over the years and the result was always the same. It was a prime site for a supermarket. Five roads led to the site, which was zoned for industry, not commerce. A zoning change would be needed. The owner of Bell Market, a downtown grocery store, feared that the building of a supermarket on "The Shoe" site would put him out of business. He waged a battle against the rezoning, as did several Beverly supermarket chains, and succeeded in collecting the necessary 3,000 signatures requiring a citywide election to settle the rezoning issue. Putting aside the issue that many of the signatures looked to have remarkably similar handwriting, the judge declared them all valid. The election was held and more than a two-thirds majority approved the rezoning. Every ward voted in favor. It was a very good sign. We had an intelligent electorate that spoke loudly. The vote was taken in early 1995. It would mean that many families in the Gloucester Crossing area could soon readily walk to the supermarket. The land was quickly sold to a developer; the project was designed, approved and constructed in rapid fashion. There is still today an active and busy Stop & Shop on the site.

1994 had flown by. The City Council was in session until late July and began again in early September. There was a lot going on. We met the need for additional learning space at the Cove Elementary School by leasing portable classrooms. The state authorized the reopening of the Community Development Office in September, freeing up $700,000 of funds for city use. We reduced the cost of ambulance services to the city by meeting with possible providers. The current provider then voluntarily reduced the cost to the city. We obtained an annual financial contribution to the city from North Shore Music Theatre, but not without argument. I was convinced that the theatre was not a totally charitable entity. Peter Seamans began work as my Administrative Assistant with funding paid largely by the Commonwealth.

The Beverly Common was often a mud bowl. Council President Bruce Nardella led the effort to create a plan for the beautification of the Common by sponsoring a best design competition. The results were exciting and a winner was chosen. Of course, we couldn't implement the plans now because we had no money but we would do so over time when we could afford it.

I learned that every time we had even a modest rainstorm, flooding of basements occurred throughout the community and I was struck with the magnitude of the problem. It was a miserable task to go to the scene of the latest flood and be able to do nothing but offer sympathy and platitudes to people with waist deep water in their cellars.

What can you do when you have no money? I have mentioned earlier our desire to create an area for business development that we could point to when people inquired about prospective development locations. One possible opportunity was a large parcel in North Beverly, which was zoned for industry but lacked access. In early 1995 two brothers, Sal and Mike Fonzo, visited me at City Hall. They owned a sophisticated machining company, Aero Manufacturing, and had outgrown their existing location in another community and now sought a site that would facilitate expansion. Their discussions with a local banker focused on a property located within the large North Beverly landmass that the bank had repossessed. The bank was anxious to sell the parcel for a modest price.

Analysis by the city indicated that the entire large landmass could be improved by building a road about a mile long across the site, improving and expanding water service to the area and providing city sanitary sewer service. The entire cost of the roadway and utility improvements was estimated at $4,000,000. These improvements would also benefit the city-owned Beverly Airport (abutting the large landmass) that was not connected to the city's sewer system.

The city had no funds to accomplish this, but our very capable and hardworking City Planner, Tina Cassidy, was well aware and knowledgeable of grant programs funded by the state to aid economic development. Tina had worked as Beverly's City Planner for several years before I arrived on the scene. Working closely with the state we secured grants of $1,350,000 for a Public Works Economic Development Grant (PWED) and $750,000 Community Development Action Grant (CDAG). That would pay for half the project.

The land that the Fonzos were ready to acquire was much larger than their current and future needs. It would be made considerably more valuable than their purchase price by the frontage on the new road and the installation of utilities. The Fonzos committed to paying the city $1,600,000 from the sale of the excess land. The Axcelis Company, a large Beverly employer, which owned land that would gain frontage on the new road, committed $225,000 to the project. The Airport also committed to a modest contribution.

When all these pieces were put together we had the funds to finance the entire project. Still there was a problem. We had no access. Marshall Handly, the City Solicitor, was able to negotiate a "friendly taking" with Tom Flatley, a noted developer, who insisted only that the area being opened up be kept to the same construction and architectural standards which his abutting area, Cherry Hill, had established and maintained. The project took time to get going. There was considerable opposition from people concerned about the environment. I found that every project of size begets opposition. We had started discussions in early 1995. It was 1998 before construction actually started, but it was a good example of long range thinking.

The Fonzo brothers asked for only one thing: that the new road be named after their father Sam Fonzo. We were happy to accommodate them. It became Sam Fonzo Drive.

In July of 1995 I hired John Dunn to replace the Collector/Treasurer who had resigned to take a better paying job in the Beverly School Department. John came from the world of finance and banking. His hiring was one of the best decisions I ever made. Right from the get-go I hoped John would be the person to replace the Finance Director I had inherited once John had time to get fully acclimated. John had a terrific talent to get things done while respecting all the rules. He got along well with everyone and he worked countless hours.

> **John Dunn**
> As fair a man as you will ever meet. John was for a time a bank executive. Later he worked on large equipment leasing. Many finance directors tell you why you can't do this or that. John had a talent for finding legal ways to get things done leaving all parties satisfied. An extremely hard worker and team player.

About this time Peter Seamans, my Administrative Assistant, requested a transfer to another position. It was very clear that newspaper reporters had been told by their editors to dig for controversy. Peter was peppered with questions that weren't his cup of tea. He was transferred to the job of administrating the city's several cemeteries. It was a quiet job but an important one which took advantage of Peter's attention to detail. Dan Murphy, who had been an executive in the newspaper industry, replaced Peter. Dan saw the good in everything and had no trouble dealing with the questions from newspaper reporters. Dan's motto was, "Always take the high road."

In 1995 the subject of flooding raised its head as it would every year until major engineering solutions were diagnosed and implemented. After a bad storm I specifically remember being in a home in Beverly Farms on Goodwin Road where one lady had mounted her washer and dryer three feet off the floor in her basement to ward off the impact of frequent floods. The lady pointed to a cellar window located close to the ceiling that she had opened to let the water out a day earlier once the flood level outside the house began to drop.

It quickly became clear to me that many houses had been built where none belonged. The presence of roofs, driveways and streets had covered much of the landscape with impervious surfaces. The Conservation Commission and the Planning Board had not existed when many development decisions had been made.

During 1994 and 1995 several prospective buyers of the entire "Shoe" parcel north of Route 62 came forward. I met with and toured the site with each of them. The site had now been essentially abandoned for seven years and it was a giant ugly eyesore. Black & Decker (B&D), which had taken over Emhart, was the owner. B&D was spending several thousand dollars each day on insurance, minimal maintenance and heat, taxes and security, etc. B&D was ready to practically give the site away to stop the cash drain.

The sum of $500,000 was bandied about as the prospective purchase price for the entire 88-acre site which included both the upper and lower ponds as well as the McKay school building built by the United Shoe Machinery Corporation in the early 1900s. Numerous people can raise that amount of money. My concern was that whoever purchased the site must have the means and the vision to take on what would have to be a massive reclamation project. In my mind my task was to discourage those suitors for whom the task was just too big.

There were several. I discouraged them all. One of them is worth a mention. The man who owned a number of low-end bargain outlet stores under the "Building 19" name spent a day with me touring the site. He talked about making "The Shoe" his flagship and largest store. I feared that the site would become a long term dump and actively discouraged him. Saving the site for someone who could really handle it was my goal.

In late 1995 the phone rang in my office. It was Tom Alexander, the go-to attorney. He said he had Bill Cummings in his office. I had never met Cummings but was very aware of who he was. I said I would be right over and joined them in a matter of minutes.

Bill Cummings went right to the point. He was soon to close on the purchase of the entire parcel north of Route 62. He intended to apply for Tax Increment Financing (TIF) after the purchase but would not make it a condition of the purchase. I told him I would support his efforts to obtain a TIF and recommend that the City Council vote favorably on the matter.

It was a special moment. I knew that the future of "The Shoe" would be transformative if a capable party with the vision and the financing was to be the buyer and I believed Bill Cummings could fit that bill.

Cummings was to pay $500,000 for the site and agree to spend $1,000,000 in environmental cleanup costs. The main complex alone contained 1,500,000 square feet of space. There were several other sizable buildings. He would be acquiring all for less than $1.00 per square foot.

Bill Cummings
From humble beginnings he rose to be a highly successful real estate magnate, seeing value where others did not by purchasing distressed properties at bargain prices. He then improved those properties to unlock their value. Bill came to Beverly in late 1995 and took on perhaps his greatest challenge by purchasing the massive rundown United Shoe Machinery complex. He was warmly greeted by the City of Beverly, which granted him a ten-year Tax Increment Financing (TIF) agreement that postponed full value real estate taxes for ten years. The city had to wait patiently for those ten years before receiving the full amount of real estate taxes due annually.

In late 1995 it was election time. Jack Monahan who had been knocked out in the primary in 1993 was my opponent. There was no primary in 1995. My election was overwhelming. I received the largest share of the total vote I would ever receive. I even joked with my friend, Mayor Peter Torigian of Peabody. He had no opponent that year but the percentage of blank votes in Peabody was higher than the percentage my opponent received in Beverly.

Getting back to Cummings and the prospect of Tax Increment Financing (TIF), the subject has another name that is more informative. It is called the Patient Capital Theory. Real estate taxes continue to be paid annually on the site but to encourage a developer to maximize his or her investment made subsequent to the purchase cost, the city agrees to not apply real estate taxes to the value the later investment creates for a number of years. Free of that tax burden, the developer invests more early on. When the period of the agreement ends, the property is taxed at its full value and going forward it is as if the agreement had never existed. TIF programs are an example of thinking long term versus the short term and I very much favor that approach.

In early 1996 Bill Cummings came forward with his TIF request. He promised to invest at least $13,500,000 in the site on the following conditions. In calculating the property valuation, Beverly would agree to exclude the entire increase in value created by Cummings's investments made subsequent to his purchase for a full five years. Further, for another five years only 50% of the increase in value caused by his investments would be recognized in calculating the property valuation. After that, real estate taxes would be paid on the full value of the property.

My first reaction was to quibble a bit, but I so wanted him to think big that I presented his offer unchanged to the City Council that unanimously approved the TIF. The relationship with Cummings was off to a very good start. Cummings proceeded to move forward. To give a sense to the size of the project, he replaced 1,700 very large windows (each approximately fifteen feet high by eight feet wide in size) around the entire plant and invested many millions more than his commitment. He pulled many dozens of building permits, generating significant unbudgeted cash flowing into the city's coffers. All of Beverly was in his corner and wished him well. The TIF would be in effect for ten full years after which Beverly would enjoy real estate taxes based on the full value of the massive site.

During 1996 the last of the inherited deficit was eliminated. Better management, tight purse strings, increased revenues, and careful hiring all contributed to this result. Beverly was on its way "Back From the Brink."

During 1996 Bill Cummings offered to donate land as a site for the new elementary school. I walked the land with Bill and suggested changes in the lot lines he proposed. The changes to which Bill agreed shrank the size of the school parcel somewhat but made certain that Cummings would retain sufficient land to later construct a new building overlooking the upper pond. Several years later Bill Cummings erected the flagship building known today as the 500 Building on that site. It is the nicest and tallest building on the campus.

Later in the year James McKeown, President of Cummings Properties, died very unexpectedly. His death came as a real shock. As mentioned earlier, the McKay School located close to the new school site had been part of the purchase of "The Shoe" by Cummings. It had been built in the early 1900s by the United Shoe Machinery Corporation and named after a pioneer in shoemaking. To honor the McKeown name, Bill Cummings offered to donate the McKay School to the city if we would name the new school "The McKeown School". We were happy to do that.

In January of 1997 the City Council voted to accept the 6.5-acre parcel of land donated by Bill Cummings for the new school and voted to appropriate the sum of $6,659,100 for its construction. The size of 6.5 acres was required by the Massachusetts School Building Authority (MSBA) to ensure state participation in paying for the new school.

The superintendent of schools had decided the size of the new school with two classrooms per grade. Years later when we faced severe school budget issues, the small size of the school turned out to be a severe handicap.

With the McKay School back in the fold, it played a key role in the elementary school upgrade and enlargement program. Once the McKeown School was complete and in service, in each year that followed one of the five remaining schools would be emptied and undergo renovation. The children from that school would spend that year in the McKay School. Once the new school was built, the program started with the Ayers School, followed by Hannah, Cove, North Beverly and Centerville in that order. The process worked very smoothly. Construction was finally completed in 2003.

Before discussing more about 1997 there are several initiatives in 1996 in need of mention. In that year we began a citywide study to identify and plan solutions to our flooding problems. These existed in five of the six wards in the city. We didn't have the financial resources to deal with them yet but we were able to begin to identify solutions.

In August of 1996 we held a big party on the newly completed Beverly/Salem Bridge. One side of the bridge was closed off completely and filled with a huge crowd. The Beverly Citizen headline read, "Tens of thousands turn out to dedicate the Beverly/ Salem Bridge." The crowd was large and the music loud. A couple of times we had to stop the music when the bridge began to shake. In the course of the festivities I met an elderly lady who told me, "They have been talking about building this bridge since I was sixteen." I asked, "How old are you now?" She responded, "Eighty-three."

The new bridge made access to the McDonald's Restaurant on the Beverly side difficult. A spokesman for McDonald's told me, "Ours are not destination restaurants." The restaurant was closed soon thereafter. With significant help from the State of Massachusetts, the city was able to purchase the Glover Wharf site where McDonald's was located.

On a scary note, in November of 1996 the original Briscoe School at Ellis Square in the downtown went up in flames. The fire was spectacular with flames high in the sky. One man told me later that he had seen the fire while driving on Storrow Drive in Boston. A general alarm was sounded. We had firefighters on the roofs of all the buildings in a circle around the school pouring water on the roofs. It was windy. Had it been windier, who knows how bad the outcome might have been. When I finally arrived home, having been a day long spectator, I had burn marks through my clothes from tiny flying embers.

Fortunately, the flames were finally brought under control. The building at the time was empty and it was thought that homeless people had started the fire trying to keep warm. The interior of the building was wood construction that burned out completely. The brick exterior of the building remained intact and the building was later reconstructed as a senior living facility.

By the end of 1996 John Dunn had been on the job as collector/treasurer for eighteen months and was ready to take over as the finance director. Don Young, the incumbent finance director, was let go to the surprise of no one and we changed the locks on the doors at City Hall. John Dunn was confirmed by the City Council in January of 1997. The vote was unanimous except for that of Councilor Peter Gilmore, whose opposition was a sign of things to come.

A very proud moment occurred in March of 1997 when Bill Cummings presented me with a framed and autographed sketch of the Cummings Center as seen looking at the south face from Elliott Street after improvements. The introduction pages of this book show the sketch and his appreciation in words for what Beverly had done to aid his progress.

Now turning to organizational issues. Until a few months earlier I had left totally intact the day one organization I had inherited. Observations over time convinced me that significant change was needed in the Public Works Department. I had the fortunate benefit of having been the Public Works Officer at the Naval Supply Center in New Jersey. It was a job I understood.

The Beverly Public Works Department had seen many positions be filled by patronage over the years. People were hired who lacked essential qualifications. It was a case of whom you knew rather than what you knew. As a result the Department had many unskilled workers, forcing the city to resort to hiring outside contractors time after time for relatively simple problems. That meant Beverly was repeatedly paying twice to accomplish a task once. At that time the Director of Public Works and Director of Engineering positions were served by the same person, who spent most of his time in his City Hall office, a mile away from the Public Works buildings.

In July of 2006 I split those duties and appointed Mike Papamechail to the position of Director of Public Works. He was an ex-marine, a successful contractor with a broad mechanical background and a terrific work ethic. I knew the quality of his work. Mike shook up the troops. He set a powerful example. He could assess a man's skills in a very short period of time. Naturally there was a backlash. Change is difficult.

On April 1, 1997 there was a snowstorm. More than a dozen Public Works employees called in sick in an effort to embarrass both Papamechail and myself. The ability to fight the storm was greatly impaired as a result and it showed. Our performance was poor. At City Hall we sent everyone home early that day and only Linda Giallongo, my executive secretary, and I stayed in the building.

That afternoon the phone rang off the hook. Linda and I shared the calls. One lady called who said she lived in southern New Hampshire and that she had driven through Beverly on her way from Boston to home. She went on to say that all the roads were in great shape except Beverly's, which were terrible. I wondered why anyone would drive through Beverly to get from Boston to New Hampshire and then I got it. I had the wife of a Public Works employee on the phone. I received numerous other calls that were obvious setups.

The storm was a tide turning event. We held a number of heart-to-heart talks in the aftermath. People had to get with the program or move on. Later in the year in November when a severe storm struck Beverly, the snow plowing performance was excellent. Change for the better had occurred.

Papamechail put in four good years, from 1996-2000 and engineered tremendous change in skill levels and work attitudes. A large percentage of the employees turned over; many retirements took place. Papamechail left in the year 2000 and recommended Mike Collins to replace him. Collins had been working in the Salem Public Works Department. References and interviews showed he had multiple strengths. The decision to hire Mike Collins turned out to be a very good one. Collins had deep roots in Beverly and simply wanted to do the best job he could. The Public Works Department became increasingly skilled and productive. Our need to hire outside contractors for simple jobs disappeared.

Mike Papamechail
An ex-marine, a successful mechanical contractor, a good judge of people's skills. He possessed a strong work ethic and passed it on to others. He had a tough exterior but a warm heart.

Mike Collins
Young, energetic, forward thinking. Up to date on the latest engineering, technology and communications advances. Very thoughtful and measured in his responses to issues.

Also in 1997 the Director of Engineering and I came to agree that his looking for another job would be best for everyone. He resigned after finding a new position in another community. Shortly thereafter in June I was fortunate to hire as Chief Engineer Frank Killilea who had many years of experience with the well-known engineering firm, Metcalf and Eddy, on large projects throughout the whole world. His expertise would be very valuable as we pursued flooding solutions.

Morale was very poor within the Police Department. I interviewed at length more than eighty officers individually. All but three members of the entire force agreed to speak with me voluntarily. Almost all the officers had lost confidence in the Chief. I wanted to remove the Chief from his position but because of Civil Service protection I could not. The recently enacted City Charter provided for the position of Commissioner of Public Safety to which both the Police and Fire Chiefs would report. It took time but I convinced the City Council to create this position and approve the appointment of Ken Pelonzi, the Fire Chief, to it. The Police Chief was so upset with this appointment that he resigned as I had hoped he would. It was April of 1998 when he left.

One more comment about organizing city departments.. The number of positions reporting directly to the mayor well exceeded a dozen. Books on organizational theory usually recommend a number from five to seven. The reason is that when the number of reports is too great, there is not enough time to give people adequate face time. Over a period of time I had observed that Beverly's Library Director, Tom Scully, was extremely capable and a talented manager. I took the unusual step of creating the position of Director of Community Services and appointed Scully to supervise Veterans Services, Recreation, Senior Services and Youth Services and the Health Department as well as the Public Libraries. That arrangement, while unusual, worked very well because of Scully's talents. When he later left the city's employment, I had to revert to the original organizational format despite its shortcomings. I did not have an adequate replacement.

Some Last Minute Opposition

As the year went on there was no talk of any opposition in the upcoming mayor's race. We had a lot going on, most of it quite positive. There were critics of my hiring Papamechail to run Public Works, but I was very happy with the progress I was seeing. We had done no campaigning and raised little money. It looked as though I would get by unopposed. On the final day to take out papers to run I checked with the Clerk's office just before noon and to my great surprise Phil Dunkelbarger had taken out papers earlier in the morning.

I was caught completely off guard. Dunkelbarger had been quietly preparing his campaign. He had run for mayor unsuccessfully five times in earlier years and had a base of support. He no doubt had support within the Public Works Department where some people objected to the new businesslike atmosphere. Dunkelbarger ran on the slogan "Take Back Beverly" depicting me as the outsider. The position of mayor was looking more interesting to possible contenders now that Beverly had eliminated the deficit and its bond rating had increased.

It was very hard to start campaigning in the middle of the summer with little money in the campaign account, but we scrambled and became very active. Tom Alexander, a lifetime Beverly resident, had lived through all five of Dunkelbarger's earlier campaigns, every one of which had predated my involvement in politics. He helped create a mailer depicting Dunkelbarger's promises to voters in each of the earlier elections. We sent a copy to every residence in the city. The mailer was very effective. It hit home.

There was no primary. The campaign was contentious. In the end we prevailed with 54.8% of the vote to Dunkelbarger's 45.1%. Our margin was four votes short of 800. That was relatively close.

With the election over and successful, it was time to reflect on important happenings in 1997. First, let me tell you about one activity which resulted in good luck, the Washington Beadle School. We were planning to close the Washington Beadle School but Mother Nature closed it for us. The red brick schoolhouse had not had any repointing of its brick exterior for many years, if ever. The phenomenon of warm days and cold nights causing a freezing then thawing cycle over many winters eventually worked its way into the mortar between the bricks and bricks fell to the ground from the archway over an entrance. One morning we found several broken bricks lying on the ground.

The school was located at the intersection of Route 62 and Route 1A, better known to all us as the corner of Elliott and Rantoul Streets. Walgreens had shown an interest in the site for a drugstore. On a weekend day I happened to visit my sister and brother-in-law in nearby Burlington. I only saw them every few months but today was the day. My brother-in-law, Frank, was a member of the Planning Board in Burlington. I mentioned to him that representatives from Walgreens would be visiting me at the office on Monday to discuss the school site. The normally very laid-back Frank responded quickly, "Oh those 'censored,' whatever they say they will be lying." He had personal experience with Walgreens. He went on to tell me that Walgreens had a book on site selection used throughout the United States. Their number one goal was to locate on a numbered route. Even better was to locate on two numbered routes at a crossing. The situation in Beverly was perfect at the intersection of Routes 62 and 1A.

On Monday morning one of several Walgreens representatives said, "We are interested in the site. It is worth six figures but only a modest six figures." Armed with what Frank had told me I said, "If it is not worth seven figures I suggest you folks leave now." No one got up to leave. Walgreens eventually paid $1.7 million for the site as well as the costs to demolish the school. The entire site measured 1.03 acres.

With the recent scary fire near Elliott Square fresh in my mind, I pushed for an emergency declaration to tear down the empty school and avoid the prospect of another fire. I received pushback from more people than anticipated, but proceeded with the immediate demolition for public safety reasons.

In 1997 the state was improving a long stretch of Route 62, Elliott Street. The construction was naturally causing traffic problems. Kevin Sullivan, the state's Secretary of Transportation and a former mayor, called one day and offered to put out a contract to improve a major section of

Route 1A in North Beverly. He said it might be many years of waiting to get that job done if we did not take advantage of the opportunity to do it now. I decided to go forward with the job now knowing that many drivers would be upset with two major road projects going on simultaneously and they were.

Bill Lupini, the newly appointed Superintendent of Schools arrived in time for the fall term in 1997. Everyone greeted him with open arms, myself included. His predecessor had been an embarrassment. Bill Lupini was young, energetic, well spoken and intelligent. When he arrived the school budget for Fiscal '97-'98 was already in place.

In 1997 we also made the improvements called for by the winning proposal of 1994 to beautify the Beverly Common and the results were stunning. We did the job on an industrial strength basis. It ran a little over budget but it was worth it. To this day I find it inspiring to look at the Common as I pass by.

Studies had shown that 35% of all the water pumped into Beverly's mains from the reservoir was unaccounted for; in other words, we didn't know where it went. There were two obvious culprits, leaks, and usage we could not measure and thus free of charge to the user. To combat leaks we started to listen at 3:00 a.m. with stethoscopes for the noise of water moving through large pipes when all should be quiet. That became an ongoing effort.

The other issue was tougher. Huge numbers of water users were being sent estimated bills. Gaining access to people's homes and businesses to read meters was very difficult, if not impossible. Some people were gaming the system.

We began a remotely readable water meter program that called for a new and modern meter in every home and business. All of Beverly could be read in short order by a small van driving up and down every street at ten to fifteen miles per hour reading all the meters electronically.

This was a big effort that took several years to complete because it required access to every home and building. It uncovered a variety of problems. It was a source of contention when it resulted in large bills for past usage in some cases, but it was entirely necessary.

Now moving on to 1998. Early in the year Pauline Teixeira joined the Human Resources Department and began close inspection of health care costs. Her detailed investigation showed that money was being wasted. Health care premiums were being paid to insurers for a number of people who no longer worked for the city. Indeed, in several cases premiums were being paid for people who were dead. Fixing these problems obviously aided city finances.

In April Superintendent Lupini presented his school budget for FY 98-99 requesting $31.5 million, an 11% increase. Lupini was quoted saying, "I'm the first one to say it's not realistic (that we'll receive it all)." The city did manage to provide $30 million, some $600,000 more than the state required be spent and a full 6% increase in our largest budget item. I was pleased we were able to do it.

The McKeown School was opened. It had been finished just in time. It was well received. It was the first new school in Beverly in over thirty years. The contract to improve and enlarge the Ayers School was signed and construction started.

After receiving all needed approvals construction finally began on Sam Fonzo Drive and utility improvements in the adjoining North Beverly area.

The "sweetheart" arrangement for operation of the golf course, which had been shoved down my throat back in 1994, was to expire at the end of 1998. The State of Massachusetts now insisted that such projects be evaluated using the Request For Proposals process (RFP). It was my first experience with that evaluation system which demanded a response of not only how much; i.e., how many dollars a respondent was willing to pay, but also a qualitative response as to how well the proposed arrangement would meet the city's needs. That meant the award would not necessarily go to the highest dollar bidder. The anticipated quality of the golf course management could also be considered. My task was to assemble a group of persons to evaluate the responses and choose the best one.

The natural group to do the evaluation was the Golf and Tennis Commission. While the "King and the Prince" were still members, the

> **Pauline Teixeira**
> Low key but very knowledgeable of human resource issues. A competent negotiator and a calming voice. Good at getting down into the details of issues.

group was large and included many fair minded people. I anticipated a fair determination. Unlike the deal of five years ago all the responses offered real money for the right to operate the course. The recommendation came back to me that we award the contract to the current operator, Friel, and we did so.

Soon another respondent, Johnson Turf Management, headed by a Mr. Douglas Johnson, sued the city challenging the award. The City Solicitor recommended we take the matter to arbitration, which we did.

During the earlier process of analyzing RFP responses, the entire commission had met with Mr. Johnson. The discussion was contentious. He had told the members that he did not have to answer their questions. When it came time for a vote by commission members to make their recommendations, not one of the eight votes cast was in favor of Johnson.

Notwithstanding the above, the matter was now in the hands of the arbiter who determined that the award should have been made to Johnson. That decision was final. Under the settlement the city had to pay Johnson's legal fees and accept a reduced sum for the first year of the contract.

The city and I received a lot of negative publicity. Almost lost in the shuffle, the good news was that after many years of the city receiving a pittance for granting the privilege of running the golf course to an operator, the city was finally on a trajectory to receive significant six-figure annual payments from the course well into the future.

In retrospect, while I had replaced several members of the commission prior to the evaluation of the pending contract, I should have replaced more of them. I believe that part of the contention with Johnson during the evaluation process was due to entrenched commission members determined to have it their way which meant a continuation with Friel.

Moving now to 1999, in January the City Council approved $5.3 million to cover the cost of capping the 30 acre Brimbal Avenue Landfill, known to many as the city dump. Beverly had been ordered to cap the landfill some thirteen years earlier in 1986 by the Massachusetts Department of Environmental Protection.

The order was ignored by the city for all that time.

Eight bids were received; the lowest of these was $4.135 million, which was accepted. This was a straight monetary bid project open to qualified bidders, not an RFP.

In 1999 we were finally ready to take on major drainage problems with real projects. The City Council voted $9 million of bonding in January to pursue the first three of what eventually would be five major projects. The approval of the funding for the three projects was monumental. The problems had existed for decades, in one case for nearly a century. In order, they were first Chase Street in the downtown, then Lawrence Brook in the Cove, and finally, Chubbs Brook in Beverly Farms.

The elevation of the Chase Street area was so close to sea level that at high tide in the Bass River the water in drainpipes actually flowed in the wrong direction up the pipes for a distance instead of down into the river. The piping was a rat's nest with illegal connections and right angle turns, something to be avoided in drainage systems. The solution, after improving the entire pipe layout, was to install high capacity pumps near the river capable of emptying out a residential swimming pool in a minute or so. Given that electricity outages often occur in times of flooding, these pumps were equipped with emergency generators.

The second project, Lawrence Brook, was a classic big pipe layout in Ward 4 from end to end. The existing system was simply undersized. The third effort to improve Chubbs Brook in Beverly Farms involved the creation of detention basins upstream that then would drain out in a controlled fashion down to the ocean over a period of time.

In April of 1999 Superintendent Lupini brought forward his proposed budget for FY'99-2000 requesting a 15% increase of $5 million, an impossible target. I was quoted saying, "The schools will get a lot of new money but this is an increase of 15% over last year's spending and we all have to live with Proposition 2-1/2." I was all for spending as much on the schools as we could afford.

We had built a new school and were upgrading and enlarging an elementary school each year. The debt service on these schools was being carried outside the approved school budget. I was disappointed by the massive request, but I had no choice but to defend what was possible. It put a strain on our relationship.

1999 was an election year. In the 1997 race, Peter Gilmore had been elected President of the City Council. He had become a constant critic of mine starting in January of 1997 when he cast the lone dissenting vote on the appointment of John Dunn to be the city's Finance Director.

Fortunately, I had always been able to maintain a strong positive relationship with most of the City Councilors. Gilmore had done his best to help Dunkelbarger in 1997 and now in 1999 Gilmore threw the whole weight of his position into helping him again. Dunkelbarger thought that coming fairly close in 1997 could be translated into a win in 1999. He chose to run on the subject of excess sewer charges to users in Beverly. He had no case. In fact, Beverly's charges to customers in comparison with those of other cities and towns, and the statements of ratings agencies, including Moody's, showed him to be wrong. I wrote a personal letter to every Beverly resident explaining the subject in detail and in November, instead of coming closer, Dunkelbarger lost by a far greater margin than he had in 1997. Soon Dunkelbarger moved out of town and Gilmore who had chosen not to run for City Council went to the sidelines. I was doubly pleased.

Late in 1999 the death of a North Shore man by freezing in the cold weather in nearby Salem was front page material in the Salem News. As a mayor I often asked myself, "What is the worst thing that could happen today?" My answer on this day was, "I don't want someone to freeze to death in Beverly on my watch."

By now the city owned the empty McDonalds building on the waterfront. I knew if I asked for permission to employ it as a shelter, I would not get it; someone would object. So I didn't ask, I went ahead and opened the McDonalds as a shelter until the winter weather ended. I knew I would be criticized but I have often been criticized. I believe that was the only time in my years as mayor that I acted as an autocrat. Some might disagree. The good news was that no homeless person froze in Beverly. Most people in the community were pleased that those less fortunate had refuge.

Moving to the year 2000, the long range plan of the School Committee had for years been to improve the middle schools when the elementary program was complete and save improving the high school for last. After all, despite its problems the high school was decades newer than the Briscoe School.

One night at a School Committee meeting early in the year it was suddenly clear from the conversation that the batting order had been changed. The high school would come first. It was immediately obvious that private off-line discussions had been held, which did not include me.

I was neither happy nor unhappy with the switch in priorities. I didn't care which school came first because I intended to see all schools be improved, but I realized that School Committee meetings were becoming perfunctory. Decisions were being made outside the meetings. It wasn't long before the reason for the change became evident. The superintendent was in discussions with New England Association of Schools and Colleges (NEASC) regarding accreditation. It was NEASC's responsibility to review the accreditation status of all Massachusetts high schools from time to time. In September of 2000 Beverly High school's accreditation was in fact placed on "warning" status because of "large scale deterioration of the building, its infrastructure and its instructional equipment." This was a real scare.

As a result, using funds budgeted for other purposes but available to him, the superintendent funded a feasibility study of Beverly High school with an architectural firm, Symmes, Maini and McKee (SMMA). The purpose of the analysis was to provide a comprehensive examination of the current high school and to develop options and costs for future facilities needs. This report would not be delivered until July of 2002, some seven months after I left office having lost the election of 2001.

Losing, Teaching, Then Winning Again

Turning now to the year 2001 and the election, I will pick up on the feasibility study later.

In 2001 in the face of a difficult economy, the State of Massachusetts authorized a plan to shrink the size of local government. In an effort to induce employees to retire early, cities and towns would be allowed to credit employees either five years of additional service or five years of additional age in calculating pensions. Either approach generally added about one-third to a person's pension. A person who had been eligible for $45,000 yearly would see that number rise to approximately $60,000. Beverly would be eligible for 25 such early retirements. The program had real appeal to some employees.

If the people being pensioned off did not need to be replaced, the retirement plan was clearly a good idea, but in Beverly's situation I believed we would need to replace nearly every one of these people. In that case not only would our ultimate pension costs involve two pensions, we still would have a salary to pay as well as the medical cost coverage of both the pensioner and the new hire and their families. I took a firm stand against the program. It was not in the financial interest of Beverly to approve it. We had only recently "Brought Beverly Back From the Brink."

My opponent in the election of 2001 was Tom Crean who had readily agreed, if elected, to endorse the early retirement plan.

The night before the election I left the office about 6:00 p.m. and walked toward the Council Chambers. As I approached the doors, the lights in the Chamber were on and the room was packed with people, including Tom Crean and Peter Gilmore. There must have been a hundred people in there. Most of them appeared to be city employees. They were organizing, I believed, for the next day's sign holding at polling locations. I turned around and went the other way.

I knew the election of the next day would be close. Families, relatives, friends and perhaps some coworkers of those seeking the early retirement plan would support them. I expected low turnout and that would not help. This was election number five for me and the incredible support of volunteers from earlier elections had waned. Everyone who has run for office multiple times will agree that the enthusiasm of supporters declines with time. It is only natural.

My strained relationship with the school superintendent would not help. The golf course issue was probably a net negative despite the fact that we now received serious money annually. And, let's face it, some people just didn't like my mother's little boy.

We lost the election the next day by very few votes, 245 to be exact, but we lost. In my opinion, the single biggest reason we lost the election was my position on the early retirement plan, which Crean implemented immediately after he took office. I was disappointed of course to lose, but I believed I had done a good job. I had dug the city out of a big hole. The deficit was long gone; the bond rating had been increased five times. I couldn't feel badly about doing what I believed was right. I had little to say as I left office.

What would I do with myself next? It wasn't long before I received an offer to teach at Endicott College as an Associate Professor. My educational qualifications were decent and my life experience was broad.

I wondered if I would be a good teacher. I would try. I was done with politics. I had no intention of trying to get back in. It turned out that I was a good teacher. I learned that the job involved a great many hours if one wanted to do it well. I enjoyed interacting with students and finding different ways to reach them. I had gone to college with brilliant professors who could not teach worth a damn. They didn't try to find different ways to reach students.

I stayed totally away from local politics in 2002 but Louise and I did continue to read the newspapers. Right away Tom Crean started blaming me for all sorts of things, day after day. Crean had chosen Peter Gilmore to be his solicitor and he too joined in to cast verbal rocks at me. In the summer of 2002 with the college closed from June to September, I actually took Jack Monahan's earlier advice and took the summer off. I built a stone wall in my yard. Soon Crean was back at it impugning me. At a point near the end of the year my wife Louise turned to me one day and said, "You have to run again and beat Crean. He's never going to stop blaming you for everything." Soon numbers of people were encouraging me to run again, and the bumper sticker slogan, "Bring Back Bill" was born.

After a time, I came around and made the decision to run again. I announced my intention at a gathering held on April 1, 2003 at the Vittori Rocci Post. I picked that date in part because of the humor of announcing on April Fool's Day. That night the room was packed. It was the largest crowd I have ever seen in that hall, estimated at 500 people. The audience was charged up. The air was electric. "Bring Back Bill" resonated throughout the room. They wanted me to come back. It was a good feeling.

The job I had done over eight years was now more appreciated than it had been when I left office. Crean was floundering around getting nothing done. His failed performance made me look better every day. Losing the 2001 election to him had actually become the best thing that ever happened to me politically.

Returning now to the feasibility study of the high school. Of course, I wasn't present in 2002 and 2003 having lost the 2001 election, but I believe the following to be accurate. In July of 2002 SMMA issued a lengthy report with four options. They all had similar price tags of about $50 million in 2002 dollars.

One option was chosen and as a result an order was put before the City Council with strong support from the superintendent to authorize spending of $734,000 for design drawings leading to long term renovations. The caveat was that even with the recommended costly improvements the useful life of the high school would only be extended eight to ten years after which a brand new school would be needed.

In April of 2003 the Council voted 5-4 against spending the money. Approval would have bought time with NEASC. Disapproval made certain the high school would be put on "probation." Probation was one step closer to loss of accreditation and that was not good news for anyone in Beverly, especially the superintendent.

Also in April of 2003 Superintendent Lupini received a six year contract extension and a vote of confidence from the School Committee. At the same time it became public knowledge that Lupini had recently been a finalist for the superintendent position in nearby North Andover.

Getting back to the campaign, Crean continued his verbal assaults; he spread the word to the newspapers that the FBI was investigating me. When questioned the FBI issued its standard answer, "We will neither confirm nor deny." In fact, my son, also a William, was undergoing background checks as part of the process of becoming an FBI Special Agent.

In the May/June period Crean had found himself unable to build a balanced budget. Local aid, the return to communities of some of the money paid by people in those communities to the state in the form of income taxes and fees, had been cut by the state late in the budgeting process. The loss in local aid for the fiscal year to Beverly was $3 million, thus creating a very real problem.

Crean tried to do two things in a hasty fashion. He attempted a home rule petition allowing him to unilaterally increase employee health care contribution percentages. His action incensed many employees and soon went nowhere. Following that he tried to impose a poorly thought out trash fee which was voted down 7-1 by the City Council in late June. The new budget year began July 1st.

In the September primary I received 3,080 votes to Crean's 1,732. I was very confident as we approached the final vote in November. In October Louise and I traveled to Quantico, Virginia to witness young Bill being sworn in as an FBI Special Agent by Robert Mueller, then Director of the FBI.

In November the vote went in my favor 6,250 to 4,365 for Tom Crean. On election night at the Rocci Post around 10:00 p.m. most of the crowd had left and I was talking with Michele Gordon, who had just won the Ward 2 School Committee race. Superintendent Lupini had terminated Michele months earlier from her position as Director of Food Services for the Beverly Public Schools.

As we chatted, who should walk in but Bill Lupini. We three talked amicably for about a half hour. At that point the superintendent said goodnight and left. I wondered what he was thinking? I was not surprised when he announced months later that he had become the superintendent in Brookline, Mass.

In the weeks between the election and the swearing in, I spent time thinking about my return to office. The election of 2003 was for me a new beginning but one with eight years of experience. During those years I had been very much focused on Beverly's problems with little involvement in regional or statewide issues. I had not been involved in policy making.

I had participated in the Massachusetts Municipal Association (MMA) but only modestly. Now I had an opportunity to think more broadly. Not many mayors get elected five times, thus I was already one of the senior mayors in the state. I would think more regionally. I would be a strong supporter of the effort to build a new regional vocational technical high school for the North Shore. I would pursue a seat on the Legislative Council of the MMA, a group that met in Boston once a month in the morning and then walked up Beacon Hill in the early afternoon to meet with the Governor or Lieutenant Governor to discuss important issues.

These were plans I made and would carry out but the immediate problems were all about Beverly. The two most important issues were avoiding an operating loss and holding on to the high school's accreditation. No one knew what the loss of accreditation would do to housing prices in Beverly. Estimates ranged as high as a 15% drop.

Some people favored pursuit of an override to raise funds. I did not pursue that idea because it would pit the financially strong against the financially struggling. I completely agreed with the City Council vote of April 2003 against appropriating $734,000 to fund construction drawings. There was no point in pursuing an 8-to-10 year solution. We needed a long term answer. Not even mentioned in the reasons put forth by NEASC for pursuing the loss of accreditation was the fact that the current high school had eleven different floor levels. A physically challenged person would never get truly equal access in that environment. The answer had to be an entirely new academic wing, hopefully incorporating the existing field house and auditorium into the design.

On his way out the door at the end of 2003 Tom Crean awarded himself nearly $7,000 in vacation pay and paid $100 for a city-owned computer that he declared surplus. A Superior Court Judge would later rule that Crean had to repay the vacation pay to the City of Beverly. He was also fined $1,000 by the State Ethics Commission for breaking conflict of interest laws. Crean hadn't received very good legal advice from his City Solicitor, Peter Gilmore. It wasn't too much later that Gilmore moved out of Beverly. I was not unhappy that he was gone.

74

Back At It In Tough Times

When I went back into the mayor's office after two years away, it was as if I had just been gone for a long weekend. Many files and papers were exactly where I had left them and appeared to have gone untouched.

Earlier, when I had lost the 2001 election and Crean entered office, Tina Cassidy, the City Planner, resigned, as did John Dunn, the Finance Director, and Marshall Handly, the City Solicitor. Tina had joined a consulting firm; John had become the Finance Director in the City of Melrose. Marshall returned to full-time private practice.

As I returned to office I reappointed Tina. John resigned his position in Melrose and returned to Beverly as the Finance Director and I chose Roy Gelineau to be the City Solicitor. I also promoted Pauline Teixeira to the Human Resources Director position left open when Crean left office.

Tom Crean had forced the retirement of Linda Giallongo as Executive Secretary to the Mayor. He had replaced her with Crystal Atherton, who had been employed by the city for a number of years doing secretarial work. I reversed that process rehiring Linda and leaving Crystal without a job. She chose to retire; then she sued me. The case wound up before Federal Judge Mark Wolf who asked me, "Wouldn't you like to settle this matter?" Having thought about this question beforehand I was not interested in the word settle. It meant compromise. Linda was talented and capable; in my mind Crystal was not. I responded, "I would certainly like to get it behind me." After a time the judge's decision was in our favor.

> **Roy Gelineau**
> Lifelong Beverly native. Served the U.S. Government as a bank examiner for a time; went on to become a lawyer. Endowed with an extra large amount of "common sense," he excelled at reaching reasonable resolution of union-related issues and other matters requiring negotiations. His ability to effectively conduct union negotiations in-house saved the city very significant sums of money.

On day one I eliminated the mayor's administrative assistant position. For one thing it would save money and show that I was serious about cost reductions. On top of that I found it easier and more productive to deal directly with the news reporters who had been instructed to seek out controversy. I became an advocate for the "kitchen cabinet" approach of Franklin Roosevelt with Tina, John, Roy and sometimes Pauline and Mike Collins dealing with key issues. Often the group met on Friday afternoons in my office. City Hall officially closed at 1:00 p.m. on Fridays. That put an extra load on those folks, but I think they enjoyed the involvement.

The first place I looked to save money was at rising medical costs representing a significant portion of the annual city budget. Reviewing the roster of retirees Pauline pointed out that while most retirees had voluntarily signed up for Medicare B, about 150 of them had not. As a result, costs which the Federal Government stood ready to pay wound up having to be paid by the city. Those who had not joined were avoiding the monthly Medicare B premiums. We began an effort to make Medicare B mandatory for both current and future retirees. Naturally, those to be affected fought back and made some city councilors nervous about the vote they would soon have to take to enact the inclusion measure. With a real effort we prevailed. It was fair and it passed.

We also went to work on the employee contribution to medical coverage. For many years the city had paid 90% of the premium while the employee paid 10%. With help from action at the state level and fruitful negotiation at the local level, we were able to change the employee contribution to 20% which resulted not only in significant ongoing savings on its face but also a change in behavior in some instances because people had more skin in the game. The savings from the change were very significant.

When Bill Lupini left to work in Brookline in 2004, Jim Hayes was promoted to the superintendent position. For years superintendents had been encouraged by the Massachusetts Superintendents Association to include numbers of new positions they would like to fill when preparing their annual budgets.

That made sense, but then the superintendents were advised to refer to any new position not approved in the final budget as a cut, even though the position had never existed. It was important that we deal with facts. I asked the Human Resources staff to prepare a report to be updated twice a year, in the spring and in the fall, showing total school employment by job category to cover all the actual people on the payroll. The needed data didn't come easily, but the report was developed. From then on when we looked at next year, we measured from this year. That approach made the annual school budget preparation more straightforward and less contentious.

Another step we took of necessity was to enact a modest trash fee that cost the average family about $2.00 per week and we began to emphasize recycling strongly in our community. Every ton of recycled trash avoided a trip to the incinerator that would save us $72. That turned out to be important.

In order to make ends meet in 2005, the city was forced to merge the two middle schools into one and close the other. While the newer Memorial School was in better condition, it was simply too small to accommodate all the students. Thus, the Briscoe School became the single Middle School.

When faced with this task, Superintendent Hayes and his team did a good job. The change went smoothly. It was healthy to have all the Middle School students under the same roof. Historically there had often been questions as to which students went to Memorial and which to Briscoe. That question was no longer relevant.

Throughout 2004 and into 2005 Beverly faced the loss of accreditation of its high school and as mentioned an ongoing annual loss of $3 million in Local Aid. The Massachusetts School Building Authority (MSBA) had placed a total and complete moratorium on all new school projects across the State of Massachusetts because the program had gotten out of control. Since MSBA usually paid at least half of every project, without its contribution no project was going anywhere.

Beverly High school was currently on probation. I knew NEASC was serious and would soon vote to strip the high school's accreditation but I didn't believe the state would just stand by and let it happen. Our loss of accreditation would be a black eye for the state too. I had the sense that MSBA would open their acceptance window at least partially in 2006. I knew that Beverly's problem, namely loss of accreditation, ranked very high on the list of reasons for approving projects, only overcrowding and the combination of health and safety issues ranked higher. I also knew that NEASC had to take several internal votes before the loss of accreditation would become final.

MSBA was developing new rules and regulations to avoid the problems that had plagued the old system and caused the moratorium. I paid close attention to following MSBA's every wish.

Since no projects were being approved, architects were hungry for work. Beverly put out a request for architects on a pro-bono basis to offer sketches of their ideas for the new school and several responded. We also hired Heery Company to be the Owner's Project Manager (OPM) representing the city, as a result of a new regulation put forth by MSBA. We were particularly impressed with the response of the Mount Vernon Group architects, as was the OPM.

We were moving quickly to keep the pressure on MSBA and to demonstrate to NEASC that we were taking the accreditation issue very seriously. In the spring of 2005 I presented to the City Council a request for $3.6 million for plans and specifications for a new academic wing incorporating the field house and auditorium into the project.

In June of 2005 the City Council faced a vote remarkably similar, yet even more remarkably different, from the vote of April 2003. Now instead of funds for drawings to improve the high school and buy 8 to 10 years of service once those improvements had been made, on the table was a $3.6 million expenditure to produce plans and specifications for what was estimated to be a $60 million project that would deliver an up-to-date new high school ready to function for many decades into the future. The proposal was approved by a 6-3 vote of the Council in late June. Those councilors who had voted down the 2003 proposal to just refurbish the high school had acted in the best interests of the city. In July NEASC took its first internal vote to strip Beverly High school of its accreditation.

2005 was once again an election year. My opponent would be a newcomer named Patrick Lucci whose claim to fame was that he'd been a radio talk show host. He had certainly never seen a microphone he didn't like.

Lucci wanted to repeal the recently enacted Medicare legislation complaining it represented age discrimination. I caught him misrepresenting school department policies at a pre-election forum. He had few followers. He offered no specific solutions. The election was not close. I won handily.

Lucci had advertised on a full sized billboard near Gloucester Crossing during the election. The day after the election the billboard was being changed to advertise work boots. An observant newspaper photographer took a picture, half showing Lucci, and the other half a big boot. It was on the front page of the paper the next day. The caption read, "Given The Boot."

The election of 2005 was a vote of confidence for myself and for my plan to satisfy NEASC while working with MSBA to obtain their timely approval and maximum percentage financing of the new school. We intended to have Beverly be one of the first ten projects approved by MSBA after the moratorium was lifted.

In my inaugural speech of January 3, 2006, I announced my intention to soon ask the City Council to approve the sum of $60 million to build a new school describing the project as "absolutely essential to prevent the loss of accreditation." Here we were under continuing pressure from the ongoing loss of local aid having to commit to a huge financial obligation. But MSBA had indicated that it hoped to start approving projects in 2006 and we were in the first ten to be considered with a high priority reason for consideration, namely loss of accreditation. I liked our chances.

How would Beverly pay for the expensive new school? Balancing the annual budget had been very difficult since 2003 due to the continued large cutback in local aid. In 2005 Beverly had been forced to merge the two middle schools to cut costs.

Now I was asking the City Council to approve a badly needed $60 million project. My ace in the hole would be the arrival of real estate taxes on the full value of the Cummings Center after ten years of the city patiently waiting. As of July 1, 2007 the property would be fully taxable.

2006 saw much work being done regarding the new school. Enrollment predictions were carefully developed. I did my own calculations. It was essential that the new school be sized correctly for the future. With guidance from the OPM (Heery Corp.) we moved close to signing a contract with the Mount Vernon Group, our first choice of architects. A thorough Statement of Interest developed by Superintendent Hayes was presented to MSBA. We covered all the bases.

The proposal put forward to the City Council in early 2006 to authorize the $60 million project was soon approved. That approval came only three weeks before the final NEASC vote to strip Beverly High school of its accreditation was to be taken. NEASC accepted the Council vote as intended compliance by the city and ceased any further actions. It had been a very close call.

The process to obtain MSBA approval would take time but we were comfortable that approval would be forthcoming. Now the only issues in my mind were what level of state funding would be granted and on what date that approval would occur.

Also moving forward in 2006, the two remaining drainage projects affecting North Beverly in Wards 3 and 5 got underway. Both these projects required large diameter drain pipes in extensive areas where none existed. Once all five of the projects were complete, analysis showed that the improvements represented a very modest cost per household across the city of a cup of coffee or two per week. Houses that had flooded for years now had dry basements. No doubt the value of many homes was increased.

In 2006 we formed the North Shore Coalition of Mayors and Town Managers. The group reached from Newburyport to Lynn. I was voted Chair of the group given my seniority. The North Shore lacked a state-of-the-art, full-sized vocational technical high school. Every other region in the state had one. Our most important task was to galvanize and organize support for a new regional school. Several communities had their own schools with limited offerings and often out-of-date curricula. Regionalism was the way to go. Danvers Town Manager Wayne Marquis was very active and helpful as we pursued this objective. It took time but we were able to muster a strong regional emphasis that eventually resulted in success. We worked closely with the Metropolitan Area Planning Council (MAPC) that represented over one hundred eastern Massachusetts communities to make sure our region received its share of time, attention and money.

As we moved into 2007 the Beverly School project was one of the few leading the pack and clearing another hurdle in the quest for funding.

2007 turned out to be a pivotal year. It certainly didn't look that way as the year started. We had been struggling financially since 2003 and that struggle would continue past 2007 as the reader will learn.

At the same time the state had a new governor, Deval Patrick, a Democrat. We wondered if his priorities might differ from those of his predecessor. Starting way back in 1994, my first year in office, Tina Cassidy and I had trekked repeatedly to Boston, at least a dozen times, to lobby for a commuter rail parking garage at the Beverly Depot Train Station. Our Senator, Fred Berry, a true friend of Beverly and the most senior State Senator had connected us to senior Massachusetts Bay Transportation Authority (MBTA) officials. We were well received. Discussions were amicable. Progress toward a garage was nil. We had gotten nowhere.

The Beverly Depot Train Station was the third busiest commuter rail station in the entire state despite the fact that it provided very limited parking. Located near the junction of the Rockport and Newburyport rail lines, the Depot had the advantage of trains to and from both sources and frequent service at rush hours. People located in Beverly and in towns to the northeast of Beverly would gladly drive to the station and then take the train to Boston if parking were available. That would help by taking traffic off the main highways to Massachusetts' capitol city. The garage idea made a lot of sense.

Senator Berry could arrange meetings with anyone he wished. He had that power. At our request he set up a meeting with Jay Gonzalez, the newly appointed Secretary of Administration and Finance, to discuss the garage concept. The results were electric. Gonzalez assured us that Governor Patrick would endorse the garage project. We were delighted.

Tina Cassidy and I had also attended a great many meetings over the years to review Transportation Improvement Projects (TIP) that set the priorities for highway improvements across the state. The total upgrading of Rantoul Street in the Beverly downtown had been on the TIP list for well over a decade. Now the project had risen close to the top of the pile.

It was a back-of-sidewalk to back-of-sidewalk project (meaning total upgrade) including updating all underground utilities. I was sure its completion coupled with the commuter rail garage would result in residential development along Rantoul Street while bringing more people and more business to our city every day.

Beverly had recently revised zoning regulations at Tina Cassidy's urging, adding 20 feet to the allowable height of buildings in a defined area along Rantoul Street. That allowed for two more highly desirable upper floors in residential buildings to be constructed near public transportation.

The coming combination of the garage and the roadway improvements started a trend. People who were finding Boston and Charlestown real estate costs too high began to consider moving to Beverly and commuting to Boston by train. The public investments in the roadway and the garage would be important stimuli that would drive appropriate new growth in the City of Beverly. Once started, that new growth would persist well into the future.

As mentioned earlier, Mike Collins was hired in the year 2000 as the Director of Public Works. Soon thereafter the name of the Department was changed to the Department of Public Services because of the breadth of services provided to the community. He continued the transformation of the department into a highly competent and proud group capable of doing a great variety of tasks. He was bright, well informed, hard working and an effective leader.

The maintenance of the schools had historically reported on the organization chart to the superintendent. I had a concern that if that responsibility were to be transferred to the Public Services Department we might never be able to satisfy the superintendent with our performance. Yet, to his credit, and likely to his relief, Superintendent Hayes knew that custodians and maintenance personnel were not his cup of tea. He was open to shifting those responsibilities to the city side.

Within the schools the word maintenance had come to mean janitorial; all real maintenance meant the use of outside contractors. It was the same lack of skilled personnel that we had encountered in 1996 when the Public Works Department was reorganized. It is hard enough to develop needed skill sets in one place in the city, never mind in two. Hayes' willingness to shift the maintenance responsibility turned out to be good for everyone and cost effective.

As noted earlier, the TIF agreement between the City of Beverly and Bill Cummings, owner of the Cummings Center, was to expire on June 30, 2007. For the fiscal year to begin the next day, real estate taxes would be based on the full valuation of the property. To aid the city in establishing the value fairly and correctly, the city engaged an out-of-town professional business evaluation expert to value the complex property. The city then discounted the resulting valuation by 10% to be conservative and to try to avoid arguments. We would repeat that process annually.

Needless to say, we didn't always get agreement but that is the nature of business. Bill Cummings didn't get rich by not being a tough negotiator. The Cummings Center was the single most valuable property in the City of Beverly. It was the single best example of new growth the city needed to fund many projects. After ten years of patience, taxes based on the full value of the site had finally arrived. Bill Cummings coming to Beverly had been good for him and good for the city. We were glad he had chosen to do so, even as he worked to minimize his tax bill.

In 2007 an audit by the state of the elementary school program that had been completed in 2003 showed that Beverly was due an additional $630,000 in state reimbursement per year. This year's money was quickly put to work paving streets and purchasing a new street sweeper. In the midst of a multi-year tight money situation, the funds were most welcome.

Also in 2007, soil samples from the ball fields at Innocenti Park were found to be contaminated. The land along the river had been filled in a great many years earlier. Who knows where the fill had come from?

The cost to remove the bad soil and take it to an appropriate location would be astronomical. We then hit on the idea of a geotextile fabric covering the entire field to then be raised by two feet with clean soil. That solution brought the cost down to $830,000, of which a state grant paid $580,000 and the city paid the balance.

2007 was another election year. This time my opponent was Euplio Marciano, an inveterate candidate for different positions who had never won an election. Tom Crean made a feeble attempt to run for a third time and was eliminated in the primary by Euplio who himself was not a serious candidate. In November I was pleased to receive more than 70% of the vote.

Part of 2008 was very difficult. Those who advocated an override to provide the school system with additional funds pushed forward. As mentioned earlier, I took no position on the matter. I believed my job was to find a way to do a good job without it.

The superintendent put forward a plan to close two elementary schools in the event the override was to fail. Cove and McKeown would be closed for the upcoming new school year. Cove would become a citywide preschool. It was rare for me to miss a School Committee meeting but I did miss one because I was out of town at an important mayors' conference. I didn't expect the School Committee to take a vote on the superintendent's proposal that night, but I did ask one of the members to take detailed notes and share them with me on my return. The superintendent did in fact press for a vote endorsing his plan that night and his plan was approved.

Upon my return to Beverly on the weekend I reviewed the notes provided to me showing the superintendent's numbers. My first conclusion was that the Cove School, located on a dead end street far from the center of the city, would not be a good location for a preschool. Traffic problems would be considerable with multiple drop offs from all parts of Beverly of very young children.

Unfortunately, I could see no way to keep open the McKeown School as an elementary school. It had only two classrooms per grade. It was smaller than any of the others. Parents of the children to be moved to other elementary schools were understandably very disappointed to say the least. We would, however, find a very important and indeed essential role for the McKeown School to fulfill.

I had very recently uncovered a favorable budget variance of over $600,000 based on a successful recycling program. Every ton we added to recycling had saved us $72 by reducing the tonnage delivered to the incinerator. Tonnage to the incinerator had dropped markedly. A beneficial state regulation regarding cardboard recycling had aided our effort.

Using the superintendent's figures and by applying the favorable variance funds, I believed we could keep the Cove School functioning as an elementary school.

I announced my recommendation at a packed evening meeting in the high school auditorium and many in the crowd gasped. It was, of course, only a recommendation but the Committee chose to accept it thus overriding the superintendent's plan.

I was roasted in the Salem News by Managing Editor Nelson Benton and called the "imperious" mayor. Perhaps he thought I was trespassing onto the superintendent's turf. Sometimes it's good to have thick skin.

Several weeks later the override petition to raise an additional $2.5 million for the schools was defeated in a citywide vote 6,686 to 3,846. When we checked in the fall, class sizes had barely changed. Most people were happy. Indeed, the McKeown School would become the citywide preschool and also house central administration. Its location was very convenient. The outcome was good. We had avoided adding to people's taxes while keeping class sizes reasonable.

From 2004 into 2008, we faced a constant battle to balance the budget with lower revenues due to local aid reductions and the ongoing saga of the high school. Now in 2008 we had some definitive good news to report. The high school project would soon break ground and the state would pay 58.42% of the cost. The cost of the entire project was now $81-million leaving the city to pay down principal of $33,680,000 while the state would pay $47,320,000.

My role with the high school would now change. In many construction projects the gorilla in the room is the existence of change orders. Bids come in low because bidders see design faults that will demand change orders. I had extensive experience in the Navy Civil Engineer Corps negotiating change orders and I decided to personally review every request for a change order along with the Owner's Project Manager as the high school progressed. It was a difficult project because the school had to be kept open and functional for several years as the project moved forward. All the academic space would be new but the auditorium and field house would be upgraded. During the life of the project I would personally visit the site more than 200 times. It was a great project, well designed and well constructed, but because it was a combination of the old and new it had many little twists and turns.

Another piece of good news in 2008 was Governor Deval Patrick's visit to Beverly announcing the $18.5 million commuter rail parking garage at the Beverly Depot. His visit was added confirmation that the key project would become reality. That was very good news. We worked very closely with Secretary Gonzalez over the next several years to deliver the garage. The extreme level of assistance and cooperation from Gonzalez over those years showed him to be the most helpful and broad-minded person I ever encountered in government at any level.

On a personal note, in 2008 I was honored to receive the Theodore Mann Regional Leadership Award named after Teddy Mann who had been the long-term mayor of Newton, Mass. It is awarded annually by the Metropolitan Area Planning Council (MAPC) representing more than one hundred communities. Some years earlier, my friend the late Mayor

Peter Torigian of Peabody, had received the award and I was delighted to follow in his footsteps. As my seniority grew the regional impact of my views also grew. By now we had moved the concept of the North Shore Regional Vocational School a good distance toward reality. Construction of that project would be a plus for the entire North Shore. We needed a full-sized school with an up-to-date and broad curriculum to provide the North Shore with sufficient numbers of competent blue collar and technical workers. At the ceremony in Boston I was quoted saying, "Regionalism is not a dirty word." That went over well.

While local aid in 2009 was still lower than it had been in 2002, the new growth that I had talked about for so long began to take hold in Beverly. The parking garage at the Depot Train Station coupled with the extensive improvements to Rantoul Street after many years of talk would soon become reality. These were drivers of redevelopment. Smart money was buying up property along Rantoul Street intent on building taller buildings with more residential units. The high costs of housing in Boston and Charlestown were causing people to seriously consider moving to Beverly with its frequent train service to and from Boston.

Another Surprise Opponent

In 2009 I was extremely busy with the high school project spending part of every day keeping tabs on it. It was springtime when I learned that Ward 3 councilor John Burke was running for mayor. Burke began using his time, day after day, knocking on doors throughout Beverly.

Although Burke was the most despicable opponent I ever faced, he had a strong work ethic. He put in the time. He knocked on an incredible number of doors. He could have been an actor. He was able to make good first impressions. He had obtained from the City Clerk's office the name and address of every registered dog in Beverly and when door knocking he would mention each dog by name. Some people were very impressed when he mentioned their dog by name while others were freaked out and wondered how the hell did he know that.

Two years earlier in 2007 Burke had sent anonymous letters to each of his fellow councilors and the police alleging police cover-ups and corruption. He was found out because he accidentally left the flash drive containing all the illicit information beside a copying machine in City Hall. That's right, he used city equipment and supplies to produce his nefarious letters. The flash drive was turned over to the police who discovered its contents and exposed them.

So embarrassing and disturbing and disgraceful was the material that the City Council voted unanimously to censure Burke, to express no confidence in him and to ask for his resignation. He refused to resign.

It was important that people be reminded of what Burke had done two years earlier and alerted to what he might do in the future. I spent time making sure that people were aware of Burke's actions. There was no primary. As the November election neared more and more people became aware of Burke's past actions and his popularity faded. I won by a good margin on election night and it is true that I refused to shake Burke's hand. I said thank you when he offered crocodile congratulations, but I knew a lot about Burke —none good — which had never made the newspapers, and to me the handshake had meaning. I was called out by Nelson Benton, editor of the Salem News, for my reaction, but I would do the same thing if I had it to do over again.

Burke then moved out of town. Good riddance. It was particularly gratifying to win the race against Burke. Over the years he had done what he could to make my life difficult. During the election campaign I fortunately had the support of all the other councilors. Steady progress on the high school project was also a plus for me.

Lots Of Good News

Once again after the election, but before the New Year began, I took stock of things. Local aid for the fiscal year July 2009-June 2010 was still less than it had been in FY 2002-2003, but things were getting better. The high school was progressing nicely. The last two drainage projects were a success. They each corrected difficult situations, one in North Beverly, and the other in Raymond Farms. Engineering-wise they were not difficult but they were extensive and provided many residents with significant relief. Our efforts regarding the Regional Vocational Technical High School had paid off. A first class facility at a new location on land belonging to the state was underway. It was a very significant project that would benefit the entire northeast region of Massachusetts.

With things happening in the downtown, which would generate new growth for some years into the future, I turned some of my attention to the large landmass in and around the Brimbal Avenue/Route 128 interchange which was zoned for business. A portion of Brimbal Avenue is residential, at one end in Ward 4 and at the other end in Ward 5. In the middle near where Brimbal Avenue crosses over Route 128 there is a business district. Looked at from the sky there was a large uninterrupted landmass to both the north and the south of Brimbal Avenue zoned for business. To the north that landmass extends across Route 128 near the Music Theatre. The interchange where Route 128 and Brimbal Avenue meet was chaos. It was a traffic nightmare but perhaps it was an opportunity.

2010 was a terrific year for Beverly. Before year end the high school project would be complete. We had been able to ensure that the public project was built to private work standards. There should not be a difference but there often is one. It helped that the contractors who specialized in building schools had been starved for work during the MSBA moratorium and ours was one of the first projects to get going after the moratorium was lifted. It also helped greatly that the OPM did a good job and our own personal interest in the project was ever present.

Early in the year School Committee member Maria Decker approached me with a request. She wanted to create and file with the MSBA a full-fledged Statement of Interest for the new Middle School to be built on the Memorial School site. She wanted to get on MSBA's list early knowing it would be long. She offered to do the qualitative side of the project; i.e., the written word and asked that I pursue the quantitative component, the relevant numbers. We agreed and put together an 80-page document over a period of months, later referred to by MSBA officials as the most complete Statement of Interest they had thus far received.

It was timely thinking by Maria because after the moratorium had been lifted, huge numbers of projects were put forward for consideration by MSBA. Later it would become clear that the new Middle School achieved reality two years earlier than it would have without her early action.

By 2010 I was close to being the longest serving mayor in the state, certainly in the top five. Over the years I had been precluded from the opportunity to be president of the Massachusetts Mayors Association because nearly all Massachusetts mayors are Democrats, whereas I have been a lifelong Independent. That, however, opened up the opportunity to be the president of the entire Massachusetts Municipal Association involving town managers, finance directors, and the like, including many Republicans.

I was elected in 2010 to that position, which gave me the opportunity to rub elbows with a number of key officials. At the Annual Massachusetts Municipal Meetings held at the Hynes Convention Center, I had the opportunity to deliver an extended introduction of Governor Patrick and his kickoff speech. I included a strong thank you for the new commuter rail parking garage that was in the final design stage.

Over the years there had been much enthusiasm for a dog park in Beverly, yet every effort in that regard was met with opposition. While many people love dogs, as I do, many people do not. Finally in 2010 I had an idea. Why not build a park on the outskirts of the city in a wooded area with no neighbors to complain? The Beverly Airport had plenty of suitable land. The Airport Commissioners reacted well to the idea. It took time and a lot of volunteer effort and it was well into 2011 before the park was completed. We managed to build a fenced in area in the shape of a hockey stick. Half of the blade area was for small dogs. The other half and the stick shaft area was for big dogs and small dogs that thought they were big dogs.

Louise and I helped clear the area. We spent a number of Saturdays doing so. We got to know a number of new people, nearly all of them younger than we were. On the day when the dog park was commissioned in 2011, we found to our complete surprise that the park had been named after our golden retriever named Paddles. He had passed away several years earlier but had lived to be seventeen and a half. His name on the park was a very nice gesture that Louise and I still appreciate.

Paddles Park created another pleasant surprise. To enjoy the use of the park a dog needed to be registered. Suddenly hundreds of Beverly dogs whose existence had not been previously known were registered. The resulting fees paid for much of the park.

The new Beverly High school was dedicated in November 2010. It was a very happy event. Catherine Kraven, the Executive Director of MSBA, joined the party and during her remarks she stated that her husband had asked her, "Who is this guy the mayor of Beverly? You talk to him more often than you talk to me." That of course was an exaggeration, but it was true that she and I had both graduated from the same high school in Boston. (Boston Latin was coeducational by the time she attended.) That connection was helpful as we worked together for more than five years from the start to the finish of the high school project.

In 2011 the state offered an interesting proposal to communities across the state. Within limits, if the community could raise private funds the state would match them as funding for a needed project. In Beverly's case the project was a turf field at the high school.

This offer was most unusual. People generally feel they pay plenty in taxes. Now the state was offering to match privately raised funds. I thought the idea was novel and I put out the bait to wealthy individuals in the community. The response was terrific. In almost no time about a dozen key players contributed as much as $50,000 each and the state came through. It wasn't something I would try again but the idea had particular appeal to quite a lot of successful business people in Beverly.

My Last Hurrah

When I announced my intention to run again for mayor on February 22, 2011 while delivering my annual State of the City Address, I was the third person to do so. Both Tim Flaherty and Mike Cahill had made their announcements earlier.

Both candidates were younger than I; both came from large lifelong Beverly families; both had graduated from Beverly High school and both were experienced veterans of the local political scene. Announcing their intentions early was likely intended to send me a signal that perhaps it was time to retire. Chronologically I was the oldest mayor in the state but I was not ready to go to the sidelines just yet. I was energetic. We had just celebrated the completion of the high school project. I had recently begun efforts at the state level to pursue grant funding for a Brimbal Avenue/Route 128 interchange upgrade, which could lead to important new revenues for Beverly. That effort would have been lost had I left the scene.

While both Cahill and Flaherty would want to do a good job, neither had ever been in charge of a large budget nor an organization of any size. Still I was the guy from out of town. They were well-known locals with deep roots. I faced tough odds yet I was confident.

In the September primary each of the three of us received a significant number of votes. Cahill was first, I was second, with Flaherty a close third.

After the primary Tim Flaherty endorsed me for the final election. That was good news. Cahill and I both campaigned hard. We took some shots at each other.

Cahill was currently the City Council President and had served as a State Representative from 1993 to 2003. I had, however, the visible and outspoken support of many City Councilors and School Committee members. I won a close election by 345 votes. The win was especially satisfying because I had more work to do and the voters gave me the chance to do it. It was also a show of confidence.

The Executive Director of the Massachusetts Municipal Association had the right to appoint one person to sit on the Governor's Economic Council and he had chosen me early in 2011. Chaired by Greg Bialecki the state's Secretary of Housing and Economic Development, a seat on the Economic Council was a plum. When I attended the next meeting of the Council held shortly after my election I was greeted with a standing ovation, which was much appreciated. The state was currently soliciting applications for economic development projects from communities throughout the state. Those chosen would be grant-funded. Bialecki had a great deal of influence in deciding which communities received grants from the state. My ongoing presence on the Council gave me added leverage in promoting Beverly's interests.

While one objective of the Brimbal Avenue/128 project was to solve traffic and safety problems at a most unusual interchange, another was to open up a significant landmass already zoned for business but lacking access. There was ample reason to believe that a commercial shopping center with a Whole Foods store as the anchor tenant would soon follow the improvements.

Interchange construction costs which included twin round-abouts and drainage improvements had an estimated construction cost of $5,000,000. Beverly was seeking the entire amount as a grant from the state. A City Council vote changing the zoning of the land in question would be required for the project to proceed. The zoning change was soon to become a major sticking point.

As 2012 began the Brimbal Avenue project took over the news. Here was an initiative which had the potential to put close to a half a million dollars in the city's coffers each year but support for the project was anything but unanimous. The Beverly City Charter contains a provision which provides for a citywide vote on a zoning change if 3,000 or more Beverly citizens sign a petition requesting the vote. Henry's Market in North Beverly had been a successful business for many years. The owner of the market was very much opposed to the prospect of Whole Foods as a competitor. The leaders of the opposition to the Brimbal Avenue project and the Henry's Market owner found each other and set up an arrangement whereby every person who went through the cash register checkout at Henry's was met with a volunteer saying, "Please sign this petition whether you are for the project or against it. We are gathering signatures to put the issue on a citywide ballot." It was a clever approach. While I did get calls at City Hall from people who felt pressured and uncomfortable, the opponents of the project amassed plenty of signatures, well more than the 3,000 needed to put the issue on the ballot. The opponents' plan was to win the vote, thus nixing the zoning change and killing the project.

If the state were to make the $5,000,000 award, it would be contingent on a favorable vote to make the zoning change. My plan was to receive the $5,000,000 commitment in grant money from the state and then win the vote to trigger the zoning change.

The opponents worked very hard and spread their concern of massive traffic problems on the Internet. They developed strong support in Wards 3 and 5. One opponent of the project with whom I spent several hours discussing the matter in my office then reported to the newspapers that I refused to meet with him.

To add to the drama, in November of 2012 the state awarded Beverly a $500,000 grant for detailed design of proposed infrastructure improvements. That was a very good sign that the $5,000,000 in construction funding would follow, but would be conditional on winning the zoning change vote.

In my mind there were significant similarities between this project and the vote back in 1995 discussed earlier when two-thirds of all the votes cast across the city were in favor of a zoning change from industrial to commercial on the "Shoe" property south of Route 62. As a result of that vote, a highly successful supermarket was built which remains busy today.

As a civil engineer I also believed that the new roadway layout utilizing twin roundabouts made terrific sense. I predicted that most traffic would come and go from Route 128. I did not believe local roads would see major traffic increases.

2013 would again be an election year. I would soon have to make a decision whether to run again for the eleventh time. I was now seventy-three. I thought about why I had run in the first place and what my goals had been. At the beginning of it all I had stated, "As mayor I would have a chance to improve things, to do some good, to make Beverly a better place, to put the city on a healthy financial trajectory and to always take the long view of the city's best interests in making decisions."

Now nearly twenty years later it was time to review the results. The deficit was long gone, the bond rating had been increased multiple times to a highly desirable level. The city's finances were in good order. The five major flooding projects were complete and successful. The schools had all been upgraded, save one, and that one, the Middle School, had been teed up. Importantly the financial trajectory to pay for the future had been established. The Common had been made beautiful. Public Services had been markedly improved in terms of skills and effectiveness.

There were still many things to be done. We had not been able to pave enough streets, but the trend was in the right direction. We had not been able to deliver a high quality restaurant on the McDonald's site. The Police Station was still a problem and the Public Service buildings needed improvement, but there would always be things that needed doing. Overall, I believed we had largely accomplished what we set out to do.

If I chose not to run again, I knew that my successor would be inheriting a strong and capable organization and need not be worried about finding people on the health insurance rolls who didn't work for the city or who had died and were still being insured. In the nearly ten years since I had returned to office following the "Bring Back Bill" campaign, department head positions had been remarkably stable. Back in 2011 Chief Engineer Frank Killilea had retired. I had combined his job and that of Public Services Director. Mike Collins had performed well and had demonstrated that he could handle the combined duties. He deserved the promotion. His title in the new job was Commissioner of Public Services.

One difference between now and what had existed when I started back in 1994 was that Collins' principal office would remain in the Public Service buildings where the bulk of the employees were located. Back in 1994 the incumbent had worked from his office in City Hall far from the center of activity.

In April I announced that I would not be a candidate in the upcoming election. I was a lame duck yet a busy lame duck. It would take at least the balance of the year for the Brimbal Avenue project to be decided. The commuter rail parking garage was nearing completion but would not open until 2014. At the time the prospect of a regional dispatch site was under serious consideration. Its adoption would require many internal communications improvements in Beverly and much time was spent planning for them. Interest in the initiative that I had personally favored would wane after my departure from office.

With my original goals largely met, it was time to step aside. Rightly or wrongly, I thought that my remaining a strong advocate for the Brimbal Avenue/Route 128 project as a bystander during the campaign would make Beverly citizens more inclined to vote in favor of the initiative and that gave me comfort.

The back and forth debate on the Brimbal Avenue/Route 128 Interchange project continued. It was not until December 13, 2013, less than three weeks before I would leave office, that the $5,000,000 grant was finally awarded to the City of Beverly — conditional on a favorable vote on the zoning change proposal to be taken in February of 2014. The news of the award was the headline in the Salem News for everyone to see. People had to ask themselves why would we turn down $5,000,000? You don't get an offer like that every day!

In the final days in office I reflected on the ten years since the "Bring Back Bill" election of 2003. A decade had passed quite quietly. I noted that the department head I spoke with most often was the City Solicitor Roy Gelineau. Nearly every move or decision had a legal angle. Roy was expert at avoiding problems and knowing when the use of outside counsel was appropriate.

Roy had a talent for injecting common sense into what appeared to be complex legal issues. The only time during his ten-year tenure that a lawsuit stood out was the Crystal Atherton matter on which the city prevailed.

The team of Roy Gelineau, John Dunn and Pauline Teixeira had handled all cityside union negotiations in-house during the ten years after my return to office in 2004. I was always on the sidelines available as necessary. Nearly every city employee is a union member. Naturally, our team had access to outside experts as needed but those resources were typically not brought to the negotiating table.

Not having expensive outsiders at the negotiating table was a tremendous benefit to the city in terms of saving money and encouraging a productive attitude in the mind of every person in the room. When union members negotiating for themselves sit across from outsiders costing hundreds of dollars per hour, it is only natural for the union members to resent the lost dollars that could be going to their fellow workers and themselves but instead were going out the window.

Several years before I left office, Linda Giallongo had chosen to retire after many years of dedicated service as the Executive Secretary. I was fortunate to hire Martha Lewis to fill that position when Linda left. She kept up the practice of providing remarkably good constituent service, always with a smile. I had made a very good choice.

As is often the case, the new administration made several changes to key positions replacing the planning director, the finance director and the city solicitor, all of whom had resigned. I was very pleased that Tina Cassidy immediately became the planning director for the City of Woburn while John Dunn equally quickly became the finance director for the City of Gloucester. Roy Gelineau returned to private practice. Pauline Teixeira and Mike Collins continued in their present roles in Beverly.

I retired on the first business day in January of 2014. On the day in February when the citywide vote on the Brimbal Avenue project was held at the high school, I held a sign for several hours as a private citizen in favor of the project. Those opposed to the project were voting against the needed zoning change. That result would kill the project and nullify the $5,000,000 grant. Despite losing the vote in Wards 3 and 5, people in the other four wards quietly flexed their muscles and voted for the project. Their votes carried the day. The project would proceed. Beverly voters had come through again. Years later it was clear they made a good decision. Traffic problems were solved and the shopping center was a success.

In the early summer of 2014 Governor Patrick came to Beverly to dedicate the newly completed Parking Garage. I was invited to the ceremony and I spoke thanking the Governor. Without his support there would have been no garage.

In the last few months before leaving office there was talk of giving me a going away present. I had discouraged that but said that if supporters of mine wanted to fund a clock to be located on the city Common as a gift to all the citizens of Beverly, I would be very pleased. On July 9, 2014 the clock was dedicated with a small plaque saying:

"A Gift to the Citizens of Beverly From Friends of Mayor Bill Scanlon, Beverly's Longest Serving Mayor, 2014." When I drive by the clock it always brings a smile to my face.

Of Special Tribute

There are two men, both now deceased, who deserve much credit for the resurgence of Beverly in the timeframe covered by this book. They are Dick Wylie and Steve Dodge.

Dr. Richard Wylie

Known as Dick to most people and as Doc Wylie by the students on campus at Endicott College, he became President of the College in 1987. When he arrived, Endicott College was a two-year women's institution in poor financial condition with declining enrollment and a bleak future.

Wylie changed all that over the next thirty years, making Endicott a successful four-year coed college which also featured graduate programs. He was a bundle of energy with lots of good ideas. Along the way Wylie created hundreds of good jobs and initiated major new construction resulting in an unexpected steady flow of building permit fees to the City of Beverly. The economic impact of the college's renaissance was huge.

Wylie also began the practice of making significant annual six figure contributions to the city. While he didn't specifically call the donations Payments in Lieu of Taxes (PILOTS), these amounts were real, significant and annual.

When Beverly had no room in its public schools for pre-K classes in the early 1990s, Wylie made space available on the Endicott campus at no cost to the city.

When it was the City of Beverly's turn to hold meetings of mayors from across the state Wylie provided space and food on-the-house, along with a presentation of Endicott's strengths for them to take back home to their cities.

It was Dick Wylie who donated "see through the smoke cameras" to the Beverly Fire Department. Leftover food from the Endicott College cafeteria regularly found its way to churches and other locations throughout the city and into the mouths of the hungry.

While Wylie was a big thinker, he was also a master of the small gesture. He knew many of the thousands of Endicott students by name, and quietly helped many of them through tough personal or financial times.

At a dinner in Wylie's honor one night to celebrate his many contributions to Beverly, I borrowed a line the people of France had used to describe their revered General Charles de Gaulle. I spoke of Dick Wylie as, "Un grand homme grand" (A physically large man with great contributions to the community.)

Wylie's passing was a great loss for Beverly and his contributions have made a lasting impact.

Stephen B. Dodge

Steve Dodge was a very successful entrepreneur. A graduate of Yale University he successfully completed OCS (Officer Candidate School) and served as a U.S. Navy Officer for several years aboard a destroyer. In an interview in 2018 Dodge said, "I did more learning and growing up in the Navy than anywhere else — before or since."

After military service Dodge took a job as a Loan Officer with the Bank of Boston. Loan requests from the infant industry of cable television soon crossed his desk and he became enamored of the budding opportunity. He chose to launch the start of his own cable company, American Cable Systems. That was to be the first of three successful cable TV related companies which he founded.

It was the year 2005 when Dodge founded his fourth company, Windover Development, and began the construction of high quality residential housing near the Depot train station in Beverly. That was the first time that Steve and I, as mayor, crossed paths. We developed a very good relationship. He was focusing a lot of attention on Beverly. He was aware of our improving situation with our bond rating having been raised several times.

Steve would visit City Hall from time to time. At one session I mentioned to Steve my concern regarding the Montserrat College of Art. The city had recently aided the move of the college to the former Hardy School building located adjacent to the Beverly Common. Montserrat had successfully responded to a Request for Proposals (RFP) put forward by the city to acquire the public property and emerged as the new owner.

I told Steve that the Montserrat College of Art was on shaky ground financially and that enrollments were down. If the college were to fail the downtown would resemble someone with several front teeth missing. Not good. Steve listened. He was a very good listener.

In the days and years which followed Steve became an "angel" to the college. Money, time, energy and management skills were given to the college by Steve and his company, Windover Development. The design and building of dormitories provided room and board to the students and money to the college. Windover was the contractor on the project and acted in a generous manner. Who knows where the college would be today if it were not for Steve's help.

Steve's contributions went beyond the college. He became a member of the Board of Directors of the Cabot Theater and devoted his time and talent along with significant financial contributions to the renaissance of the Beverly landmark. Soon Windover Development was active at the theater doing significant construction work at very reasonable costs. Steve was generous; he was also a savvy businessman. A healthy Beverly downtown helped create a healthy environment for an improving community.

Steve's demise by being fatally struck by a car while he crossed a road in Florida with his bicycle came as a terrific shock. He was in the prime of life with so much more to offer.

Thanks to Steve Dodge, Beverly is now a better place.

Photo Essay

The pages that follow capture moments in my personal, business and political life, with emphasis on the latter. There are also photographs representing the history of USM (The Shoe) at various stages and its eventual redevelopment. It's always good to reflect back on one's life experiences through photographs and I believe you will agree.

U. S. Navy Officer Candidate School, Newport, RI, 1962.
A few weeks into the OCS program each candidate was photographed wearing a dress white tunic and an officer's lid. The photo was taken in the event the candidate was to graduate. The photo was no guarantee at all that the candidate would do so. To get that point across, the picture was taken from above the waist, while the candidate wore no trousers, just his skivvies. I often wondered whether my eyes gave anything away.

Bill and young Bill Scanlon on a skating rink in Montreal, Canada.
Young Bill went on to be the better hockey player by far.

FBI Honor
My son Bill was sworn in as an FBI Special Agent in October, 2003 by then FBI Director, Robert Mueller.

Marathon Runner
My daughter Barbara is shown crossing the finish line at the Boston Marathon in 2008.

Family Get-together
Daughter Barbara (far left) with her children (left to right), Taiyo, Ellis, Anna, grandfather Bill Scanlon, and Maya.

"The Shoe" Under Original Construction:
Workers sitting on the reinforced concrete frame of a building at the United Shoe Machinery's Beverly Complex in 1908. The open spaces were to be filled with very large windows.

Photo courtesy of Historic Beverly archives.

Company Assembly
Part of the 5,000-person workforce at a United Shoe Machinery Corporation company-wide event, held in the good times.

Photo courtesy of Historic Beverly archives.

Aerial view of the vast United Shoe Machinery complex.
The main buildings were a quarter mile in length.

Photo courtesy of Historic Beverly archives.

September 22, 1993 Photo reprint courtesy of Salem Evening News

November 3, 1993, the day following my first election.

Photo reprint courtesy of Salem Evening News

Bill and Louise Scanlon with Bill's parents, on Election Night 1993.

Bill Scanlon, his father, and Salvi Modugno (right) on election night, 1993. There is a sidebar mention of Salvi on page 39.

"Scanlon: City Must Pull Together"
January 4, 1994;
my inaugural speech.

Photo reprint courtesy of Salem Evening News/
Beverly Times Photographer: Barbara Kennedy

May 18, 1995: Airport Connector Road Project to create economic development and add new tax dollars.

Photo reprint courtesy of Salem Evening News

Abandoned and derelict for too many years, Cummings Properties began transforming and modernizing of the former "Shoe" in 1996.

Photo courtesy of Historic Beverly archives.

Ultimate Revival: Aerial view of Cummings Center in 2016.

Photo courtesy of Beverly Community Access Television (BevCam)

Horrific fire at the site of the old Briscoe High School at Ellis Square in downtown Beverly, November 1996.

Photo reprint courtesy of Salem Evening News
Photographer: Paul Bilodeu

Photo courtesy of Historic Beverly archives

January 4, 2006: The push for a new Beverly High School.

▶ Beverly inauguration

Scanlon pushes for new BHS

Mayor says he will ask council for $60 million to build school

BY PAUL LEIGHTON
STAFF WRITER

BEVERLY — In an inaugural address in which he vowed to steer the city through difficult economic times, Mayor Bill Scanlon opened his record-tying sixth term yesterday by calling the construction of a new high school "absolutely essential."

Scanlon said he will ask the City Council by early February to spend about $60 million to build a new school. The New England Association of Schools and Colleges has said the high school, due to its poor physical condition, will lose its accreditation unless the money is approved.

"Passage of this important appropriation is absolutely essential to ensure that Beverly High School retains its accreditation," Scanlon said.

PAUL BILODEAU/Staff photo
Mayor Bill Scanlon delivers his address during Beverly's inauguration ceremony in the auditorium at the former Memorial Middle School yesterday.

Photo reprint courtesy of Salem Evening News
Photographer: Paul Bilodeu

How great was 2008? In addition to construction for the new high school, Beverly received backing from the state for a parking garage at the downtown train depot.

Gov. Deval Patrick came to Beverly in June to announce state backing of a new parking garage for Beverly Depot. Flanked by Patrick and U.S. Rep. John Tierney, D-Peabody, Mayor Bill Scanlon spells out the plan.

Photo attribution: © Beverly Citizen — USA TODAY NETWORK   Staff Photo: Robert Branch

The new Beverly High School was completed in 2010.

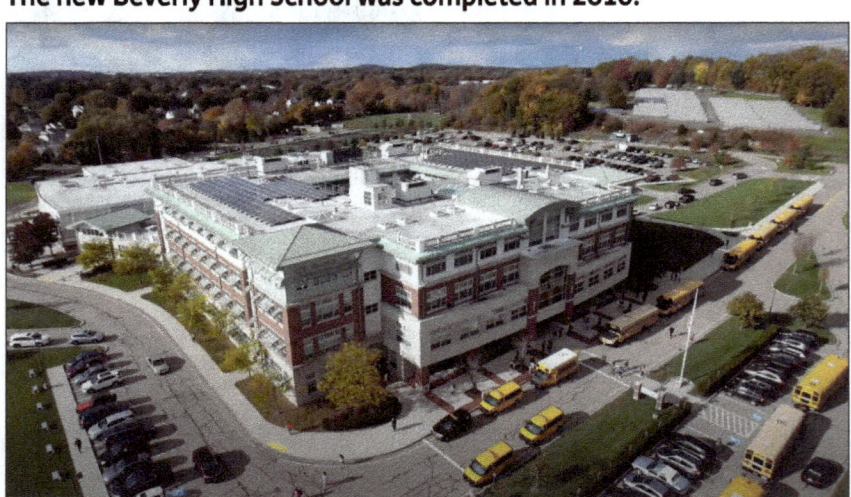

Photo courtesy of Beverly Community Access Television (BevCam)

September 15, 2011

Photo reprint courtesy of Salem Evening News
Photographer: Ken Yuszkus

2011 Election Night victory.

Photo attribution: © Beverly Citizen — USA TODAY NETWORK
Staff Photo: Kirk R. Williamson

I was sworn in as mayor for the ninth and final time on January 4, 2012 by Salem District Judge Michael Lauranzano, a Beverly native who once served as an assistant city solicitor.

Beverly Mayor Bill Scanlon, center, takes the oath of office from Judge Michael Lauranzano, left, as the mayor's wife, Louise, stands by his side on the stage at the Inauguration ceremony at Beverly High School yesterday.

Scanlon sworn in for 9th term

Nine councilors, six school board members also inaugurated

BY PAUL LEIGHTON
STAFF WRITER

BEVERLY — In 1994, Mayor Bill Scanlon took his first oath of office in the Beverly High School auditorium.

Yesterday, that same loca-

Scanlon urged the City Council to "continue to have an open mind" on accepting new growth opportunities.

auditorium and this building look so good."

Scanlon's speech capped an hourlong ceremony that also included the inauguration of nine city councilors and six School Committee members.

Photo reprint courtesy of Salem Evening News   Photographer: Ken Yuszkus

December, 2013: The state approved of the project and voters followed suit and did likewise. A Whole Foods market now serves as the anchor store for this North Beverly plaza.

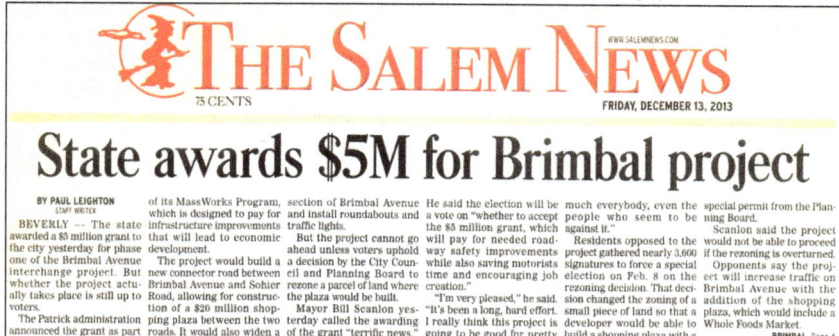

Photo reprint courtesy of Salem Evening News

July 7, 2014: My comment was, "Not my clock, but our 'clock'."

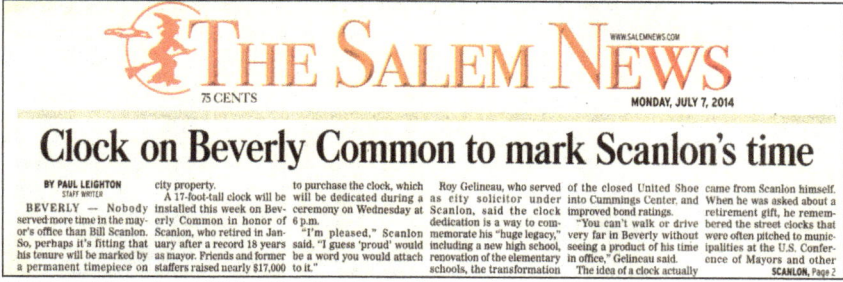

Photo reprint courtesy of Salem Evening News

Remembering our dog "Paddles" at city's dog park near the airport.

Acknowledgments

My wife, Louise, deserves kudos since my running for mayor was her idea in the first place. Her frequent inputs and suggestions during the writing of the book were very helpful and her nimble fingers produced iteration after iteration of the book before arriving at the finished product.

I especially need to reference the contributions and guidance of Lee Yaffa. I know very little about publishing, while Lee has an extensive background in the field. I thank him for coordinating the many pieces of the manuscript and photographs, enabling him to prepare and design a cohesive book I am proud to put my name to. Thanks also to Lee's wife Cathy, who in her own quiet way was a highly positive force for finding the right word or a better way to express a thought.

I appreciate the contributing efforts of Sue Goganian, Director of Historic Beverly. Sue is very talented and hard working. She and Lee often discussed publishing details that went right over my head.

Credit is due to Dave Olson, Editor of the Salem News, for his cooperation and securing photo permissions throughout the process. There are many others who reviewed the manuscript in draft stages, whose help was very important to me in composing my story.

VOTE TALLY THROUGH THE YEARS

1993				**2003**		
Scanlon	8337	62%		Scanlon	6250	59%
Gelwick	5036	38%		Crean	4365	41%
1995				**2005**		
Scanlon	9317	85%		Scanlon	5697	60%
Monahan	1641	15%		Lucci	3822	40%
1997				**2007**		
Scanlon	5143	54%		Scanlon	4356	72%
Dunkelbarger	4347	46%		Marciano	1722	28%
1999				**2009**		
Scanlon	6558	65%		Scanlon	5939	59%
Dunkelbarger	4462	35%		Burke	4105	41%
2001				**2011**		
Crean	5573	51%		Scanlon	5468	52%
Scanlon	5328	49%		Cahill	5115	48%

Beverly City Hall, courtesy of Historic Beverly, Charles Mulcahey, photographer

After accounting for publishing costs, net proceeds from the sale of this book will be shared equally by three Beverly not-for-profit organizations. They are:

Beverly Rotary Club Foundation

Maintained by the Beverly Rotary Club, which was founded in 1921 and dedicated to making Beverly a better place.

beverlyrotaryclub.com.

Harborlight Community Partners (HCP)

An entity committed to providing affordable housing in Beverly.

harborlightcp.org

Beverly Historical Society (Historic Beverly)

An organization devoted to spreading the word of Beverly's rich history dating back to the 1600s while helping shape a better future for our city.

historicbeverly.net

www.ingramcontent.com/pod-product-compliance
Lightning Source LLC
Chambersburg PA
CBHW070503100426
42743CB00010B/1743